The Collector

a memoir

Tina L. Hendricks

The Collector *is dedicated to my parents, Diane and George, and my brother, Casey.*

In writing this book, I honor my parents' story of courage amidst their pain. All the while, I applaud myself for breaking their cycle. I will learn your lessons, Mom and Dad. I will give your sorrow a voice. And, through this memoir, The Collector, *I promise to tell your truths and expose mine.*

Chapter One

The Desk

The musty smell of decades of dust greets me and I pull a long breath in through my nose. Warmth and happiness tingle through my limbs and wrap my chest in a hug. The heavy peal of a rusted bell bounces against the wooden door as I force it into a resisting doorjamb behind me.

"Good afternoon," says a woman standing on the other side of a counter constructed with grayed, repurposed boards.

"Hello," I force myself to say. My eyes meet the woman's, so I dart them away and turn my back to her. I proceed into the mass of antiquities and ignore the glimmer of an antique, nickel-bronze cash register that sits unused beside her. Such a beautiful relic. I'm curious about its story and imagine a huge price tag; however, I refrain from inquiring—making it clear that I have no desire to initiate conversation. I hope.

Once I'm sure I have avoided the harrowing and coiled trap of small talk, I slow my pace and begin to scan the clutter of artifacts. If the woman follows me, asks if I need help, or offers an "Are you looking for something in particular?" I will bark, "No," and leave if she must know where I'm from or what brought me in today.

I scan the mélange of treasures cluttering the spacious, unheated barn. A giggle, like that of a child in a toy store, escapes my throat and a buoyant array of bliss and creative intention swirls in my forehead. I welcome the artistic wave of energy that darts through my brain, settling in a focused pleasure between my ears. But it doesn't last.

The disquieting sound of two women with booming and piercing voices vibrates nausea through my chest. They browse the antique shop at the far end of a narrow path between old books and records. I turn away with a quick spin on my heels and direct myself in the opposite direction—as far from their disruption as possible. A squeal of laughter from one of them digs into my shoulder blades. I press out a forceful breath from my lungs. I blink slowly, as if I'm closing my eyes. Blackness behind my eyelids renders their noise invisible until it recurs—such an unsatisfying disruption in my salubrious treasure hunting.

I close my eyes again. I attempt self-assurance: *They cannot ruin this for me*, I repeat to myself in silence. I am my own cheerleader, and I suck at it. I know that if I'm irritated enough to call upon my self-made spirit-cheer, I'm already doomed.

My quietness—the stillness within chaos—doesn't tolerate intruders. Sometimes I flee. Today, I hope I'm strong enough to bear the weight of sharing this space with the two co-shoppers who are oblivious to my desperate need for aloneness.

I open my eyes and take in the trove of pearls surrounding

me. Scanning thousands of objects in a small space seems to bring calmness to my internal turmoil. I can see past the disarray and focus on beauty. I look up to find that the clutter continues to the ceiling. I spot an impressive chandelier hanging above me and smile.

I have concluded that the level of rarity determines the value of each unclaimed object, and maybe popularity factors in, too; however, finding a specific item that replaces a torrid memory with an imagined new one is valuable enough for me.

Today I don't know what I'm hoping to find. I rarely do. I know that looking—regardless of whether my visit ends in a purchase or not—brings me joy. Perhaps it's because I'm revisiting a rare feeling of bliss embedded in my core. Few moments of my childhood felt safe, but going to yard sales with my mother did.

———

"Oh, a yard sale," she would say, then slam on the brakes while her open palm pressed against my un–seat belted chest. We'd visit the homes of strangers and paw through their items for sale—a well-cut lawn covered with large blankets that were polka-dotted with toys, clothes, and knickknacks. We would shop for things better than our own, but only if my mom's coin purse could afford it.

Each at-home entrepreneur welcomed us onto their property with large cardboard signs and smiling faces—fathers, mothers, families, and neighbors tending to the needs of strangers. A gesture of kindness summoning financial gain and a successful yard sale for themselves.

My mother was an open book, and she inevitably shared our stories with whoever would listen. She told what, I now believe, should have been secrets. She shared them like decorations of honor she'd won from the everyday battles that made up her life.

I'd hope for a new toy: a gently used doll or teddy bear. My mother usually searched for clothes. But I remember the time when I needed bedding so clearly that it could have happened yesterday.

———

"How much for this set of twin bedsheets?" asks my mother. A woman wearing a white button-up shirt and a red money apron tied around her waist with a perfect bow joins her at a cardboard box of unmarked bedding.

The woman bends down to her knees beside my mother and paws through the box for a few seconds, then says, "How does fifty cents sound?"

"I can do that," answers my mother. She presses apart the clasp of her change purse and digs her fingers into the mass of pennies, dimes, and nickels. She squints against the sunshine and her terrible eyesight, not yet corrected with glasses. "Tarzan ruined Tina's sheets," explains my mother, as if this woman knows my father—granted, most people at least seem to recognize his (nick)name.

"He came home drunk again, and he wouldn't leave me

alone. I went into Casey's bed, and he followed me in there, so I went into Tina's bed, and he frigging followed me again. Three of us in a tiny twin bed." My mother looks up at the woman as she places two dimes and a nickel in her palm.

I look at the woman too. I wonder if she will react to what my mother said. Does she know what it means? Was my mother trying to get a reaction out of her? My guess is yes.

My mother's fingers disappear into the coin purse in search of more. Her long dark hair falls in front of her face. My mother huffs a piece out of her eyes.

"Oh." The woman stands up and turns her head toward me. "And this is Tina?"

"Yeah."

"Tina was asleep?" The woman asks my mother.

"Yup."

No, I wasn't. Just because I was quiet does not mean I was asleep. My father was drunk and pleading for something, and my mother refused, but as always, he remained persistent and desirous. I never remember what happened next. My dad following her into my bed was a common occurrence. She was always telling him, "Leave me alone, Tarzan," but he would not.

"He ended up ripping the fitted sheet with his boot," my mother adds.

"Oh dear," says the woman. She closes her fist. "Twenty-five cents will do."

"Oh, thank you," says my mother. She snaps her coin purse closed.

I go to my mother and take one of her hands. We look through the rest of their unwanted belongings while we make our way toward our car. I marvel at the downy furniture, so clean and inviting, that lines the driveway. Fluffy white pillows oozing with comfort evoke a feeling of longing within me. I realize that this beautiful furniture is unwanted. Why? Do they have something better to take its place? Is there a point in life when people don't struggle? When they are so happy and safe that they can pass on gems such as these?

"I wish we had stuff this nice," says my mother. We sink into the couch and pretend to nap. We both choke out fake snores and genuine giggles.

We climb into the dark green and rusted car. As I pull the passenger side door closed, a loud screech of metal on metal turns the heads of the other people at the yard sale. The door doesn't shut completely. I open it again, and with half of my bum dangling off the front seat, I use all of my strength to slam it closed.

My mother's first attempt to start the car is never successful. I don't worry until the third try—I hold my breath. She got it on the second try this time. We smile at each other.

"Tina, did you see that little girl? The one playing with the Barbie dolls for sale?"

"Yeah, why?"

"She was so beautiful. Did you see her looking at you?"

"No."

"I think she wanted to be your friend. She was so pretty,

and her hair was so blonde and perfect. Maybe you'll be that pretty someday."

"Yeah, maybe." We smile at each other again.

———

I pull my weighted handbag off my shoulder, which allows me to squeeze through a small space between a tall bookshelf filled with old cameras and a glass display case containing a twenty-four-piece set of yellow-rose dishes.

I spot a desk with a familiar color—light brown, almost orange. It has thick, sturdy legs and a simple square design. The top bears deep scratches from life with its past owner and has a white circle stain from the moisture of a warm cup.

The white circle pulls me in. Nostalgia rears its ugly head—a moment I haven't recalled in such detail in over forty-five years returns. I run my fingertips along the top and rub at the white ring as I try and erase the thoughts acting themselves out in my mind with the cruel intention of hurting me again. Orange and brown blurs my vision. The white circle stain spins. I become dizzy and place my hand on the desk's corner.

My mind travels far away and long ago. I can see my curly, unruly hair and tiny fingernails on the hand that hugs my dolly around her neck—freckles of pink nail polish remain and dirt colors in the edges of my fingertips.

———

My mother is crying. My God, her cries. Long, drawn, and howling. My ears haze over with numbness—ringing. I am frozen in place, unable to breathe or move. Her sadness is frightening, and I want it to stop. I want her to be silent and for her to hug me and tell me she is strong and that everything will be okay. If she isn't okay, how can I be?

What can I do? How can I make this stop? I pat my dolly's tangled yellow hair with a firmly cupped palm. My mother's cries intensify. She bellows out her sadness and pain—echoes of grief bounce against the walls of our apartment. The world doesn't hear her and no one comes to help. Instead, her children bear it all. She wants someone to know how badly she hurts. Hopelessness and fear pound out of my chest.

I put a teddy bear around one of my ears and press the opposite ear against my pillow. I can still hear her. I close my eyes and wrap my arms around my teddy and my pillow and press my biceps tight around my head. The objects under my arms close off my ears and allow me to hide.

"Stop, Mom. Please stop," I whisper to myself, wishing my quiet voice could command her. She continues. Her howls vibrate through my arms as I rope my teddy and pillow around my ears.

I pull myself up from my toddler-sized bed. I wade through the drowning sound of her cries. The air I walk through feels heavy and resistant. I force myself to press against the tide of anguish to find her. I feel lost and confused. I expect a sharp-edged knife to pierce my back, a cold hand to clench my ankle, or the face of a monster to scream out from under my bed. I brave forward.

My mother's face is red and shines with tears and sweat.

Her wails continue even though I have come to her. Her gaze lands on me but it's void of recognition. For a moment, her eyes seem to hold mine, but she doesn't see me. She looks past me and my tangled hair as if I am as transparent as the glass in a doorway. Looking into her eyes, I cannot find an ounce of love or worry for me—her frightened child—however, I absorb her jagged, pointed emptiness and it shatters me.

She paces from her bedroom to the living room and back again.

"Mommy?" I try to get her attention as she sits back on the bed. She continues to act as if I am invisible. "Mommy? Why Mommy's sad?"

My question finally reaches her. She points to a small wicker basket next to a light brown desk marred with the white circle of a water stain on the top. I find crumpled pieces of paper in the trash basket. I want her to stop crying and show me that she is going to be okay, so I pull the pieces of paper from the garbage. I unwrap their imploded edges and smooth them out on the desk by pressing my tiny straight fingers and firm sweaty palm over the wrinkles.

"I fix, Mommy." I have no idea what the words on the paper mean, but I am sure their crumpled ruin is what has her so unsettled. I continue to press my small hands across each piece and attempt to smooth away my mother's grief.

I pass them to her with a worried smile and hope to make it all better. She crumples them again in her fists and tosses them to the floor.

Her loud, long, and drawn-out calls of sadness continue.

They echo with hot heat in my ears. My chest feels heavy, my heart panicked. My entire body is devastated with fear. My knees are weak, and my limbs are numb. We are not okay—it's a world-ending feeling. I feel as if I won't survive the moment. I pull away from her and insert myself into my closet.

———

Where was my baby brother at that moment? How could I not have thought of going to him? If I was so young that I was unable to read, I too must have been a baby. Maybe on the other side of baby, when you don't wear a diaper anymore but are still a baby, nonetheless. If I was three, my mother would have been eighteen, and my brother, one and a half.

Our mother should have been preparing to graduate from high school by that time. Instead, she was a sophomore year dropout. Schooling was the last priority of hers and of multiple generations before her. Relationships with men took precedence.

The desperate edge of survival always renders my brother, Casey, invisible in my memories. Casey's presence is as absent as the hug I needed from my mother or the empathetic reassurance of her saying, "Everything's going to be okay!" or perhaps the confidence instilled in a child when her parents can take care of her.

My brother.

God, I wish I had focused on him and not her. If only I had received compassion, perhaps I would have learned to display it. As alone as I felt, he must have submitted to the lack of love and come to the conclusion that he was insignificant, as that's what his adult self still believes.

My brother is such a tender soul. Sensitive and sweet from birth. Clever, witty, intelligent, and a thousand times more handsome than the average person. He has the most beautiful jade green eyes I've ever seen and dark shining brown hair that he let me style however I wanted throughout our teenage years. His skin, unlike mine, darkens quickly in the sun, and his six-foot-three frame is the chiseled figure of an athlete.

I was alone, but Casey, he was beyond alone—isolated and lonely for most of his life. I had no idea how to show him anything else.

Remembering him as a child and knowing he was so neglected causes me horror and guilt, and the twin afflictions force an encumbrance of helplessness to pulse through me.

———

A loud "Look at this!" shouted from across the room presses an invisible tack into my palm. I look down at my fist. It's not a tack; it's my fingernails. I release their sting. I swallow the fear and insecurity that has been resurrected, as familiar as the day it happened. After a few breaths, my nerves have calmed. This awakened moment, a door opened in the corner of my mind, however difficult to relive, is mild compared to others I'm reminded of most days.

The fate of my demons is always the same—swallowed but

raging with silence behind an expression of indifference. Unchanged remembrances that only become more difficult the older and wiser I become. The more I see how wrong things were, the more I want better. Better for me, my daughter, and my husband. And my brother.

I walk away from the water-stained desk in the dusty antique store, attempting to walk away from the memory it stirred. I leave behind the first of many moments of listening to the howling cries of my mother's sadness. I recall that some years later, when I was a handful of years older, I asked my mother about that day. Although I remember asking her, and I know the answer, I won't let myself revisit the truth of what upset her that day.

The answer is here inside of me. It floats through my subconscious like a threatening storm cloud. It was never discussed again, but I carry the knowledge like a disease in remission. I don't look it straight in the eye. I hold it above me like a balloon on a string that I can't release. A balloon with an unbearable weight.

This moment for my mother was without mistake one of the many that broke her. She was never the same. This moment was a continuation of the devastation of what she was—a young girl who needed love.

I turn back to the desk and focus my thoughts on the object that unearthed this memory.

This desk is not for me. It's much too reminiscent of the one that sat in the lonely apartment in New Jersey where we were isolated, and too far away from our family in Bar Harbor,

Maine. It's far too similar to the one I used to smooth crumpled letters from the white wicker trash basket in my earliest childhood memory, the day my mother's grief pounded my soul with fear. Was that the first time I wrapped a teddy bear around my neck and over my ear while pressing my biceps tight around it and my pillow? This act of self-soothing was adopted and used throughout my childhood so often that it became the normal way for me to fall asleep. It protected me from the wars between my parents that kept me awake or shook me out of sleep. It dulled the terrifying sounds that streamed from her bedroom when she didn't close her door.

To this day, I still rope my biceps around my ears whenever I drift into sleep or relaxation. It's so habitual, I didn't even realize I did it until I began feeling resistance and pain in my aging shoulders.

I must find a desk of a contrasting color—a variance of shape with a dissimilar history. I must clothe this child within me in a fabricated apology from my now-dead mother and correct this moment in time. I must explain my way through the details and praise my older self for acknowledging this neglectful and traumatic horror.

I will cut the picture from the movie reel of memory by procuring a new desk—an antique desk. Maybe I can find a desk that belonged to a wealthy family where the children did homework and the parents paid bills, or a brilliant author wrote a novel of romance and love. I need a desk that I will use to write my stories, poems, and flash fiction. It will bring me love, success, and fortune. I will share it with my family, and it will be passed on—an heirloom of us and a broken cycle of abuse.

I will buy a desk that will become a symbol of my choice to do and invite better into my life.

My eyes begin focusing through the muddled chaos onto the tables scattered throughout the shop. There are dozens of them crowded and piled with antiquities, waiting to be found and adopted: bureaus, coffee tables, end tables, and desks. The myriad objects distracting the eye from their supportive presence disappear. I see through them. I focus on my mission of finding a desk and see nothing else.

I find her camouflaged by two lamps, a crocheted table-runner, a large vase filled with dusty silk flowers, and four hat boxes piled on top of each other. As soon as I see her, I know she's the one. She is beautiful: a dark mahogany, or maybe ebony writing desk with ornate hand carvings decorating her architecture. My heart thumps as I caress her edges and test how wiggly she is, discovering that she is solid and robust—strong enough to withstand the burden of my past.

I remove the artifacts carpeting her bosom and set them aside. I pull the heavy wooden cover down over the drawers, storage compartments, and writing space. There is an ornate metal key inside the lock, so I twist and pull it out. It is this desk's destiny to be mine. She has been waiting for me. I slide the key into my coat pocket for safekeeping—I would hate to lose the key.

The two women shoppers approach. I can feel the stinging invasion of their eyes and inquisitiveness pressing against the back of my neck. It tingles up to my scalp, and the air around me becomes sparse.

"Do you need help?" one asks.

"Nope."

Please ignore me. Go away. Pretend you don't see me. Don't hold the door, and if you must hold the door, do not expect gratitude. I don't want or need your help. Your judgment of me incurs a gesture of kindness that I am trying to avoid. I want to be left alone.

It is not that I am not thoughtful and loving. Nor that I cannot be so. Instead, my introversion is necessary for my survival. Being invisible is my shelter.

I bend my knees and press the edge of the desk into my stomach. I find a solid hold with my hands, and as I stand up, I'm relieved that the desk lifts with me. My fear and defensiveness have intensified my strength, and I'm able to carry the desk over to the woman at the register. I place it down and eye the shiny gold cash register that caught my attention when I came in. I smile a silent hello at it.

"How much for the desk?" I ask.

As if it matters. I'm not sure why I ask for the price. To complete the transaction, I must know the price—my irritability desires an efficient execution of the sale. Nothing else matters at this point. I need this desk. I won't be able to think of anything else until she is mine. I will lose sleep. I will recall the day in New Jersey to endless fatigue. I will smooth the papers over and over in my mind until I own her. I need to move forward; therefore, I need this desk.

"Three hundred and ninety-five dollars," the clerk answers.

"Okay, I'll take it."

I gently place her into the hatchback of my car, securing her over the collapsed back seats. I exhale and relax my shoulders. Contentedness releases the tension in my chest, and I embrace the calmness that my love for this object has procured.

I gaze upon the desk with affection in the same way I do my daughter, Ashlynn. I look upon Ashlynn so often, my eyes drooling with love, that it irritates her. I don't recall a single moment of feeling my mother's love by the way she looked at me. She never looked at me the way I look at Ashlynn. I see her. I see her beautiful soul, and I adore it.

My favorite photos of Ashlynn are ones when she is asleep, laughing, crying, or running. I love her uninhibited ability to be herself in these moments. I envy them.

Today, I appreciate the calm this desk had bestowed after such an overwhelming nightmare from my childhood was unexpectedly awakened. However, I'm not surprised; I know there are more lurking in the shadows of my memory, just waiting for their moment to pounce.

The journey home is tranquil. The bright sun warms the inside of the car, and the black leather upholstery cradles me as I drive. This act of purchasing a remedy—a medicine for the ailments bestowed on me from a time when the toxicity of poverty, neglect, and addiction overshadowed my life—gives me purpose.

I am a collector. I adopt heirlooms that seek shelter in dusty antique shops with hopes of finding a new home. I rescue them to fulfill my innate desire for love, and they repurpose their lives to save mine.

I fill my home with archives: remnants of a forgotten past that has been given up—someone's past—but not mine. I'm covering my ruin with a vestige of serenity and safety. I search for objects that exude longevity, family, and love.

Perhaps these objects have secrets of their own—bore witness to worse than I have—yet I can only see beauty and perseverance in their tattered upholstery and gouged edges. They will protect me from the pain of my youth. They will impart an asylum from harm: love. Material shepherds of the comforting notion of constancy and predictability: trust. History, but not mine.

I sit in my car with the new desk. Silence and the ticking of the cooling car engine soothe me further. My phone lights up—a text from Ashlynn, who is at college two hours away.

My last final is over. I can't wait to see you, Mommy. I'll be leaving in the morning.

I respond, *Congratulations! Happy summer. You kicked freshman year's butt. I'm so proud of you, and your hard work is paying off. Let me know when you are on your way home. Drive safe. See you tomorrow.*

I revisit the letters that broke my mother's heart, so split it became unrepairable. I can hear myself ask her what they said. "Mom, remember those papers in New Jersey that I tried to smooth out for you? Why were you so sad about them?" At nine years old, I was still too young to hear the answer.

"They were love letters to your father, from my sister. They'd been having sex."

"Aunt Sandra?" I ask.

"Yes," was all she said. She didn't go into detail like she usually did. Instead, she raised her hands in front of her face and began picking at her cuticles. Insistent picking followed by chewing off the loosened skin around her fingernails.

This betrayal changed my mother. It was worse for her than when she was raped at age eleven. It was the only story she didn't repeat, and the one battle scar she didn't show off. It was a pain so significant she couldn't stand to look at it. I've carried it for her my whole life.

My mother married my father when she was fifteen. She was pregnant with me, after all. My brother was born eighteen months later. They divorced when she was eighteen, but they never stayed separated for long. Through romantic relationships with other people, their jealousy remained and roared through our daily lives. It was as if they belonged to each other above all else, but neither was willing nor capable to commit to better.

My brother and I were silent witnesses to their verbal wars and infidelities. Our lives were chaos running on poverty that was never too dire for cigarettes and alcohol. There is no safe home when the betrayal of alcohol and adultery defines love.

Chapter Two

Date Night

"Cheers," I say to my husband. We clink pints of draft beer in the air.

"I love you," says Billy.

"I love you too, honey." We smile at each other and place our cell phones on the table—face up in case our daughter tries to reach us. Both of our feet dangle off the tall chairs. I rest my elbows on the bar-height table and lean in toward him. He responds, pressing his muscular shoulders forward to kiss me. For a few seconds, the noise in the juke joint section of our favorite barbecue restaurant hushes around me. He really does love me.

I inhale his cologne as I put my hand on the back of his neck and stroke the base of his short haircut. I study the multiple scars on his face. They appear in a constellation, connecting injuries around his blind right eye. When I met him, I noticed his scars, and they drew me to him. They added toughness to his otherwise handsome, innocent, and youthful look. I assumed whatever made the wounds were the cause of his blindness.

That was not the case. His brother shot him in the eye with a BB gun when Billy was five. It detached his retina. The lack of peripheral vision on his right side is what caused his facial injuries.

One long scar on his eyebrow is from a collapsed orbital bone, acquired during a rugby match. A deep laceration that now appears as a two-inch long white line across the bridge of his nose is from the edge of a metal fence he got caught up on when fleeing a college party. And there are other small scars that happened under such mundane circumstances that I don't recall their cause.

Billy is gentle, never jealous or angry. He is the exact opposite of my first husband, Ashlynn's biological father. I went from one extreme personality to the other. Billy's laid-back and loving presence is why I fell in love with him. But it's also what almost ended us. I am an adult child of alcoholic, abused, and abusive teenage parents. Laid-back and loving is not what I was used to, regardless of how attracted I was to it.

I take extra care to be aware of my cell phone. I love my husband, and I can honestly say I am finally happy; however, my happiness does not take precedence over our daughter's. A lesson learned from inattentive, self-absorbed, juvenile parents.

Ashlynn is now nineteen years old, and while she's only two hours away, she is effectively on her own. I worry and wonder about her, but above all, I am proud. She'll be home for the summer in the morning, and our lives will focus on hers.

She took a gap year between high school and college for a chance on modeling—high-fashion modeling. Ashlynn was born with the natural attributes for success in the industry—fair, beautiful skin, long dark and wavy hair, big green eyes, tall frame, and lean. Her fame skyrocketed in a short time. Her life became a rigorous schedule of trips back and forth from home to New York City, meetings with her agent, and casting calls with all of the top names in fashion and cosmetics. She landed her first supermodel-level gig with Kim Kardashian and received requests from Pink, Victoria's Secret, Maybelline, the Gap, and more.

That's when anorexia took hold of Ashlynn's good judgment and rendered her helpless to the intoxication of starvation.

I refused to let her go back to New York until she recovered, and in time she decided she didn't want to go back. She didn't want to be part of something that makes women feel the way she did—beautiful at times, but consistently never enough.

The waitress returns to our table for our order. "I'll have the pork belly tacos, a side of cornbread, and chili lime wings," I say without looking at the menu.

"And you?" she asks Billy.

"Sixteen-ounce prime rib, medium-rare, with beans and cornbread."

"You got it."

We settle into the wooden chairs at the bar-side dinner table with multiple large mouthfuls of the beer. By the time I'm halfway done with my glass, I can already feel the twinge of intoxication. My erect, uptight posture relaxes, and I can feel the corners of my eyes turn down. Alcohol is a rare beverage choice for us; however, we make time for a date night and enjoy a drink on occasion.

I check my phone for word from Ashlynn. Nothing. No news is good news with her. A single-word text reading *Mommy* is never a good sign. It's the first indication that she's struggling.

Billy and I are not always talkative on date night. Sometimes the sight of each other after a long week at work is all that matters. Other times Billy is reciprocal of conversation should I instigate. I examine his face. He isn't preoccupied, nor are his thoughts somewhere else—Billy is here with me.

However, he is a man. "You can't trust men," I hear in my mother's voice. She proved this to be true over and over. Today, I trust Billy. I will not listen to the vinyl record skipping over one firm and convincing chord of accusations upon all men in the world, which is always on repeat in my subconscious.

I press my thin, yellow, straightened hair behind my ear and take a few more sips of beer. I'm beginning to feel talkative. Billy, on occasion, will start our conversations, but most times I take the lead; however, once a topic is introduced, our discussions are vivid and enjoyable. Most times, we compare complaints about work, the struggles of publishing my book, or projects on the house.

Today, since alcohol often unlocks my rigid exterior, another chapter of hidden experiences from my childhood is revealed to Billy. He has heard so many that even I am surprised that I still have more to tell. Without a mirror, I apply the pink tip of my lip gloss wand to my lips and spread the pigment around. I return it to my purse and wiggle with eagerness to reveal more of the sickness within my family. I aim to shock him with true tales of ailments of the mind and behaviors of the broken.

"This month is eight years since my mom died," I say.

"I know."

"She was fifty-seven when she died, so that means she would be sixty-five this summer."

"She was so young when she died."

"Maybe that's why she had kids so young. I had her for forty-one years. Maybe fate was on her side at some point." Impossible. My eyes scan the ceiling of the log cabin–style building. "Do you remember when this used to be a shoe store?"

"That's right. Dexter Shoes." He examines the architecture.

"So, remember I told you we lived in New Jersey when I was like three or four?"

"One of the dozens of places you lived before graduating from high school. Yes, I remember. Why?"

"I was thinking about that apartment in New Jersey while I was antiquing today. My mom was always so sad when we lived there. It was also the first place I remember seeing my parents having sex." I look at him and wait for his reaction.

"Jesus, Tina," says Billy. "You were so young. You remember it?"

I laugh. "I know, right? Yes, I remember a lot. That was just the first time. Well, I didn't know what sex was then, but I knew it was scary. I remember being woken up by strange noises. My door was open, my parent's door was open—it was a tiny apartment. Yeah, so I got up and sat on the floor outside of my parent's bedroom, crisscrossed my ankles, hugged my teddy, and watched. They were going at it. And they were loud. I didn't know what the hell they were doing. I kind of knew, though, at the same time. But holy shit, when they saw me, they were pissed."

"At you?"

"Yeah. My parents got pissed at me because I wasn't in bed."

"That is fucked up. Couldn't your mom or dad have shut their door to begin with? I'm so sorry, honey."

"Ahh, that's nothing," I boast. I grasp my mug with both hands and sit up taller in my seat. I'm forgetting that I always regret doing this—this freedom of words and stories and this false strength I am enacting. I shoulder the fear and feel it as clear as the day it happened. Right now, I wear my trauma like a victor—just like my mother did. On occasion I display a learned habit of hers—bragging about how many wounds I have obtained, and at this moment, my collection is cataloged and honored in my mind, like a case of trophies.

I tell myself that my stories are the worst and I too have earned the right to brag. Worse than anyone could imagine, way worse than Billy's or anyone else's in the room, and because of them, I am stronger than they are. Alcohol has rendered me accessible; my shell of introversion opens, and I share a few more of my stories with the only man that I know, without a doubt, will not use my secrets against me. Even though I shouldn't trust him. Right, Mom?

I have seen men with more to lose risk it all to satisfy their desire. My father, for example. He had a woman that loved him, two children that loved him; none of us were enough for him. I wasn't enough for my father. So how could I be enough for my husband?

"And you know what else I got in trouble for?"

"I can only imagine."

"My parents walked around that apartment naked, so I took my clothes off and walked around naked too. I remember that it felt weird, but I still did it. Holy hell, I was the bad one. I got scolded for copying my family. I was trying to get their love and attention. My father, when he was around, was always mad. Drunk or sober, he was always angry.

"He would yell at my mother for letting me sleep with her, right in front of me, as if I couldn't hear him. It made me feel so insignificant. He couldn't sleep alone. Why should a three-year-old have to?" Billy shakes his head and shrugs his shoulders. I take a long drink of my draft beer, leaving only a film of foam on the bottom of the glass. "Want another round?"

"Sure." Billy catches our waitress as she walks by and orders two more drafts.

"I think that's why I stopped speaking up. Well, you figure if my father was pissed at me for seeing them have sex, I certainly wasn't going to interrupt my mother having sex with other men."

He chokes. "You saw your mother having sex with other men too?"

"Oh, hell yes. Sometimes with me in the bed." I take the fresh beer from the waitress and pass her my empty glass. The new one is cold, and the glass is frosted. I take a large gulp. "So cold. Yum."

"What the hell was wrong with your parents?"

"They were young, alcoholics, and victims of abuse themselves."

A man passing by our table stops to say hello and shake Billy's hand. I ignore this social encounter, and Billy knows not to include me. I pick up my phone and place it between my face and the man. After a lengthy and torturous sharing of pointless conversation, the man moves on.

I jump right back into my story. "After we moved back from Waterville—"

"Waterville? Weren't you just talking about New Jersey?"

"Yes, well after New Jersey, my parents got divorced and we moved to Waterville for a while. My Uncle Forrest lived there. Maybe my mother was trying to get away from my dad. I don't remember why, but I know I hated it there. It felt like a scary city compared to Bar Harbor. God, I never, ever felt safe—not anywhere."

"Your mother didn't stay anywhere long enough for you to feel safe."

"Did I tell you about how bullied I was at school there? I got kicked, punched, and teased mercilessly. Being bullied is painful. But I believed it was par for my life's course. I thought we were bad people—my family—and I just assumed that was why life was so hard. Huh, maybe that's why I turned into a bully?"

"No, you didn't tell me you got bullied. You told me about getting lost trying to walk home alone from kindergarten."

"Oh yeah, that was awful. I wore a little blue snowsuit, and a long string connected my knitted mittens through the arms of my coat so they hung out of the sleeves. It was one of those warm winter days when the snow gets packed down by the sun.

"I was supposed to walk home with a girl from our new neighborhood. It was the first damn day of school for me. Earlier, a boy had stolen my crayons because the teacher gave me brand new ones, then he kicked my knees on the playground. I cried. And I never let myself cry. I can still feel the pain in my throat from trying not to cry that day."

"Oh, honey, I know. That's so sad."

"The girl who was supposed to walk me home never came to my classroom to pick me up. I waited until it started to get dark out and the school was empty. The only thing the teacher told me to do was shut the lights off when I left. I gave up waiting for the girl, and I had to walk myself home from school. I got very lost.

"I walked so far I made it to the main drag of Waterville. Cars were zooming past. I saw an older woman, so I asked her where McDonald Street was. I looked up over the buildings and recognized the direction to my Uncle Forrest and Aunt Betty's and took off running. I didn't wait for the old lady to say anything at all. I ran in the direction of Aunt Betty's house. I was sweating so bad in my snowsuit.

"The old woman appeared worried. She changed the direction she was walking in and followed me as best she could. I kept waiving back at her and yelling, 'I'm okay now.'"

"My God, that's right. You were like five. You've told me this story."

"Yup. And the only thing I was upset about was that I forgot to shut the lights off like the teacher asked me to. I knew my mother wouldn't care about me getting lost. She would say, 'The worst that could happen is that you could die, and you didn't die, so you're fine.'"

"My God," Billy says.

"I used to knock on people's doors on McDonald Street and ask if they had chalk so I could play hopscotch." I giggle. "People used to give it to me, too."

"Sort of like when you used to call the operator and ask what time *Rudolph* was on?" Billy and I share a hearty laugh and clink our glasses together again.

"What were you saying about after you moved back from Waterville?"

"Oh yeah. My mom bought a trailer. My God, we thought it was so nice. She had quite a few boyfriends throughout her life. Let's see. I remember Jon. He was much younger than my mom, of course. I might have been in second grade by then. I think. They also had a lot of loud sex. I wanted to slam their bedroom door. I wanted to yell at them, but I never did. I would just lay there scared and furious. So I pulled my eyelashes out."

"Jesus, Tina. You pulled your eyelashes out?"

"Yeah, my mom freaked out when she saw me with no eyelashes because it looked so ugly. She took me to the doctor because she thought something was wrong with me. But I told the doctor I pulled them out. They were both disgusted with me. The doctor sent us home."

"Did you tell him why?"

"I don't remember knowing why at that time. I remember the feeling of my eyelashes coming out. It didn't even hurt. Maybe I was malnourished or something."

"Possibly, but I think it's more likely because you were dealing with bullshit."

"Sometimes when my mom was having sex with someone, I was unable to move. I felt like I was held down by some invisible force. I'd try to get up and slam their door, or yell at them to shut up, but something was holding me back. I told my mother that a ghost was holding my arms and legs down. She didn't believe me."

"It's called fear, honey."

"Oh, wait, no, there was someone else after Jon. Like, many men only came around once, but a few, like Jon, came around more often. I can't remember his name. My mom brought him to Thanksgiving dinner at my Aunt Sandra's house. I remember I drew a picture of them naked in bed, and I described the picture to the whole dinner table—they were in bed and having sex."

Billy almost spits out his mouthful of beer.

"I got in trouble and had to apologize to him. I didn't understand why I was in trouble, but I said I was sorry anyway. I think they broke up shortly after that.

"And then I remember Toby. He kept asking my mother to marry him. I remember feeling nauseous every time he asked her and then so happy when my mother said no. I could tell she liked it when he asked her, though. She would smile this weird little smile and bow her head. Her brown eyes would sparkle, and she would blink them repeatedly. My father hated him, and I was worried he would kill Toby. Somehow my dad always knew when my mother was getting ready to go out on a date, and he would come over and flip out.

"When did *Amityville Horror* come out? I remember my Aunt Sandra saying they had a secret passage to the basement and a window full of flies just like in the movie."

"I'm guessing 1979." Billy searches it on his phone. "Yup. So you were eight. You turned nine in December that year."

"Why the hell do I remember this shit? I was so young."

"Because it was fucked up, that's why," says Billy.

"I just kept squeezing my teddy bear and my pillow over my ears so I could drown out the loud sex. Oh shit, and you know what else? This was so careless of my mother, and it embarrassed me to death—my mother would let her robe fall open in front of my friends. And of course she was naked under her robe with her freaking vagina hanging out."

"Ew, don't tell me that."

"Why did men wear cut off jean shorts so short in the seventies that their jewels would hang out?"

"Um, I don't think men did that as a rule, honey."

"No? God, most men we knew did."

"What? No. Can we change the subject?"

"Okay. So I used to sleep with my mom if she was alone. If my dad or another man was there, I had to sleep in my bed. But that made me sad because sleeping with her was when I felt like she loved me, and she always blew me off when a man was around. Oh, and get this, whenever I felt sad she told me I was just feeling sorry for myself."

Billy shakes his head. I'm proud of the rise I'm getting out of him, so I continue. "I remember a few times I tried to go into her bedroom to sleep with her when Jon was there. Jon couldn't keep his hands off her."

I stop talking. The sounds of those moments return, and I can hear nothing else—their groaning and the snap of the elastic edge of my mom's underwear. The air around me thins as I recall the sheets around my neck being pulled with the constant rhythm of their movements. I can vividly recall the feeling of him tugging at her skin and the wet, fleshy sounds between them.

Screeching brakes sound inside my ears, pulling my eyes away from the blurred vision of memory that has taken over as I stare into space. I attempt to focus on Billy's face. *Tina, stop*, I say to myself. I've gone too far, and now I feel sick, disgusting, and grotesque. I don't want to remember this. Nausea pulls the blood out of my head and pushes white to my face.

Billy places his hand on mine. "I'm sorry, honey."

A spinning begins inside my head—experiences from those days stir into the spiraling funnel of a dark and aggressive storm. A cyclone of moments hurl themselves together. Out of this violent windstorm, a whipping gust makes me gasp, then another, and another—fragments from the vortex within this mega-storm of wounds erupt in an explosion of pain.

A jumble of memories from the time we lived in the trailer spin within my mind's eye. The obscene phone calls. I thought for sure it was our neighbor. He'd say awful, detailed sexual things to me. He would tell me that he was coming over and what he would do to me. And my mother's robe wouldn't stay closed when my friends were over. I know they saw the hair sprouting between her legs.

She thought everyone wanted to have sex with her. Even Harry, the older man who used to babysit us, wanted her. She wore see-through pajamas, and she would stand there, letting him stare at her, then she would tell me about it. Then I remember the night my father was nearly beaten to death. The blood. The cold unheated air, and the empty refrigerator.

I grit my teeth against the flood of unpleasant memories, but they continue unabated. I see my brother sobbing and begging our mother not to go out. Not to leave, not to choose going out to party over staying home with us. "I have to," she would say. "Jesus Christ, I'm always with you damn kids. I need to have my own goddamn life."

My eyes glaze over with tears. I take a large mouthful of beer and swallow it around the hard lump in my throat.

"Honey. It's okay. Your mother was a bitch for exposing you to that stuff. I can't believe she did that to you. She didn't protect you from anything."

"Thank you for saying that, Billy. But I still loved her. She didn't know any better."

Our food arrives. Thank goodness. I can return to quiet. I can internalize all of these ghouls that eddied out of their hiding places and put them back behind the protective walls of my blizzard-proof armor.

Why do I do this? I ask myself. I'm sure Billy would much rather talk about baseball or football or anything other than my childhood. He'd probably even prefer to have silence rather than this. My childhood was disgusting, and all I can do is relive this shit.

A vision of the first of many times I saw Jon's naked body breaks into my renewed calm as I stuff a piece of yellow cornbread in my mouth. I struggle to breathe as I try to chew through the memory. I see dirty blonde hair fuzzed over his testicles, an upward directing penis, and his indifference when he saw me. I try to ignore the visual. It's impossible.

I continue to force myself to eat. The first few bites of my pork belly tacos are difficult to stomach—nausea pulses in my chest. There is a tightness in my throat that has spread to my shoulders. My body shakes. It is hard to breathe, let alone swallow. I bring the glass of beer to my mouth, close my eyes, and take a long drink. I inhale through my nose, and the pungent smell of Bud Light snaps me out of this cyclone of ordeals.

What I share with Billy is perhaps not what I should be sharing. The story doesn't matter. The context is irrelevant. However, how I feel is. I don't share my feelings. The voicing of emotion is the hardest part, and I have no idea how to express it. I've just always kept the pain inside. It never mattered if it was physical or emotional; my pain was inconsequential.

"Have you and your brother ever talked about this?"

"No."

Casey suffered, too, but we have never talked about it.

What did he witness? Was he scared too? Did he think her sex was our mother getting hurt? Did he ever answer the obscene phone calls? What did they say to him? My mother's opinion of men was awful, yet she let them have their way with her. She allowed her body to be theirs for the taking—no permission necessary. And she hated them all for it. How could that have guided Casey in the right direction?

I exhale my internal dialogue and allow the familiar weight of regret to settle onto my chest—a lighter sentence than the punishing turmoil tattooed within me from my mother—my guilt for not protecting my brother. No matter how young I was, I should have done better.

My phone lights up. It's a text from one of my girlfriends. I hold the phone up and read her words. The food in my mouth has become dry, and I get no help from my thickened saliva. I wash the bite down with a gulp of beer. The hurricane of emotions settles, disappears—sunshine beams through the swiftly dissipating clouds.

"Kristy has a piano for me," I say as soon as my mouth is empty. I've been hoping for a piano for so long. Finally, I just may get one.

"Let me guess—she needs it moved out of one of her apartments?"

"Yes. We can have it for free if we move it."

"Why do you want a piano, honey? Neither of us play."

The blatant, thundering, vulgar sounds of my mother's lustful sex with my father and her various other men roar through my mind. A gray cloud reappears, and the whirl-wind of chaos ensues. Ear-piercing shouts of war between my parents resonate with uncanny awareness through my chest. Those were the sounds of my home.

I want the promise of new sounds. The hope of music and trust in an aged and abandoned instrument. One deserving of a place in a family that will not give up on it. A family who will continue to care and protect it long after its strings are out of tune and its wood is crackled and dull.

"I just do," I say.

"Okay."

Chapter Three

The Piano

I wake the following Saturday morning before Billy but not before our pets. I can hear our two dogs and two cats begging for their first feeding of the day at the bottom of the stairs. Billy's heavy arm lays across my belly. I caress his skin and enjoy a quiet moment with him. I am safe.

Before we can focus on our breakfast, we must tend to the needs of our animals, or there will be no relaxation for us this Saturday morning. I lift his arm and kiss his cheek.

"Don't get up yet," he whines.

"Sorry, I'm up. I'll get the animals."

Ashlynn's bedroom door is still closed. I assume she's still asleep. Ashlynn spent her first week home resting and recovering from the strains of college and the stretch of her immune system. She already misses her friends. Boredom will soon set in.

I squint against the morning sun and welcome the sound of chirping birds. Spring has arrived. My rubber muck boots sink into the soft ground as I wander through the backyard with the dogs. They follow their usual path around the perimeter, seeking out the perfect place to relieve themselves.

I'm bursting with pent-up excitement. I am beyond eager to get the piano, and I hope Billy will help me fetch it today. I know he doesn't have the same sense of urgency that I do, and I'm sure he has already identified all of the reasons this will not be an easy task—a bad habit of his.

Many times, the words "It's impossible" have exited his lips. Those words float in the air, waiting to be sucked into my lungs, disguising themselves as reality so they can quell my hopes. I do not ever use those words. I know there is always a way. The silver lining of poverty and a traumatic childhood is an unbreakable amount of empowering knowledge that I have survived worse than what most others consider to be impossible circumstances.

The dogs and I return to the kitchen. The rich smell of coffee percolating through hot water welcomes us back inside. Billy kisses me. "Good morning," he says.

I pour coffee into my tall reusable mug from Disney, add a hefty dose of cream, and two Sweet'N Lows. "What are your plans today, Billy?"

"Just the gym. Why? What's up?"

"Can we go get the piano Kristy offered me last week? Waiting this long has been hard for me."

"I knew it." He exhales a loud huff from his chest.

"Why? What? Why not?"

"Do you know how heavy pianos are?"

"No, but I know how strong you are."

"Tina, it's not that easy. We should hire a professional piano mover."

"That would mean we wouldn't be able to get it today. What about your appliance dolly?"

Knowing I will not let up, he submits. "I'll bring that too." Billy leaves the table with his coffee to sulk while he gets ready to help me.

I smile and bend down to our chocolate Lab and Old English Bulldog to pat their heads. "We're going to get our new piano today," I say in a high-pitched voice. They wag their tails and share my enthusiasm.

Billy knows how to plan for every possible worst-case scenario. He's the most capable man I have ever met. His brilliant mind earned him valedictorian status in his high school graduating class and then a doctorate in chiropractic medicine. His physical strength and hard work ethic developed from a lifetime of working his family's vegetable farm. His father and two brother in-laws were master carpenters. He'd learned everything they knew, making him a multifaceted genius.

I prepare by dressing in my at-home work clothes—black leggings and a sweatshirt splattered with various colors of paint. I grab a pair of Billy's work gloves, load my arms with as many blankets that I can carry, and meet him at the truck. He's already busy with packing his tools and attaching his trailer.

"Can't we put it in the back of the truck, Billy? Why do we need the trailer?"

"Tina, just trust me, would you?" He's frustrated, and our mission hasn't even begun yet. I'm still happy. Not happy as a child getting her way, but rather pleased as a woman settling the unsettled within her. My eagerness is a product of the desperate need to move forward.

I roll my eyes at his lack of excitement. To me, this is like going to pick up a new puppy. We are adopting a new member into our family, and I am one hundred percent certain that no matter what challenges await us, it is going to be worth it.

After Billy makes numerous trips between the garage and his truck, we are finally loaded up and ready to go.

"So, where are we going?" More frustration in his voice.

"Kristy's barn."

The twenty-three-mile drive is quiet, and I peer out the window as the sun continues to rouse the world out of its winter hibernation. We arrive just as we finish our coffees. We pull into Kristy's driveway, and I text her, letting her know we're here.

She exits the barn—a wedding venue she purchased not that long ago—and meets us at the truck. She informs us that the piano is being stored in another recently purchased property just next door.

"I've got a renter currently occupying it, but the tenant is willing to leave for a couple of hours so you can take the piano," says Kristy.

We move our truck and trailer over to the next driveway, and Kristy lets us in. The tiny square house, built in the early 1900s, appears run down and desperately in need of updating. We climb three stone steps into a four-foot by four-foot mudroom. Beyond the narrow doorway of the small mudroom, two rooms make up the first floor—a living room and a kitchen. Kristy tells us there are two bedrooms and one bathroom on the second floor.

"There it is," says Kristy.

I pull in a quick breath. "Oh my God, it's beautiful."

"Call me if you have any trouble." Kristy turns and leaves.

There she is. She has been waiting for me—an upright goddess. Her dark mahogany finish crackled with age. I open the cover to reveal the worn, dirty keys and the name of its maker in gold paint—*The York, Weaver Piano Company, York, PA.*

I look at Billy and smile. His face has softened, and I can tell that he sees the piano's beauty too. Billy grew up hearing pianos, guitars, and voices in his large and loving family, who are more musical and talented than any I have ever known. The first few times I interacted with a large group of his relatives were strenuous for me. His family, like Billy, are so generous with their love and attention. The dozens of children between his four other siblings were loud and energetic. There were a handful of times I became so overwhelmed with the chaos of activity that I had to hide in the bathroom to nurse anxiety attacks.

Now, I cherish his family and feel as if I've become a better person because of them. My prior life of solitude made it difficult for me to navigate gatherings where so many people were interested in talking with me. I've forgiven myself for the inappropriate and awkward moments of my initial encounters with them. I just hope they all love me as much as I love them.

Billy and I reach out to touch the piano's edges with our fingertips, and we've both already fallen in love.

Our first task is moving her across the small living room. It's impossible. With every push, the piano's wheels sink deeper into the dense shag pile of the area rug. After only a foot of progress, the thick pad of the twelve-by-twelve carpet has lifted away from the floor and is mounded under the pedals, acting as a roadblock. We decide the rug needs to go—a favor, really.

We push the piano back and relocate all of the living room furniture to a corner before rolling up the ancient and dirtied gold rug. The carpet is so saturated with age that it weighs more than Billy and me together, but we manage to get it out of the house and heave it to the side, albeit with a lot of effort.

Removing the carpet reveals a beautiful wood floor. Wide planks of hardwood stained a chestnut brown had been hidden and protected for years, keeping them in excellent condition despite their age.

"Shit," says Billy. "Now we have to be careful not to scratch the floor." We decide to put the piano on the rubber-wheeled rolling furniture movers that we brought. They look like double-wide skateboards. With our combined strength, we successfully lower the piano to her side on top of the rollers.

We push her toward the exit of the living room, which leads into the small mudroom—the only exit option we have.

TINA L. HENDRICKS

The doorway is too small, and the piano won't fit through it. Nor would any other average-sized piece of furniture, not in or out.

"What the hell?" Billy is perplexed. "Did they build this house around the piano?"

I am heartbroken. We can't get it out. No matter what side we put it on or the direction we attempt to maneuver; the piano will not fit. The piano is either too tall to clear the doorjamb or too wide to clear the opposite wall. My heart pounds inside my chest. I lean against the piano, darting ideas through my mind. Giving up is not in my nature. There has to be a way.

My rapid heartbeat, riddled with angst, slows, becoming rhythmic and steady. I feel my upper body being pushed away from the piano with every thump of my heart. The answer is here; I know it.

"Billy. We have to take down a wall to get it out, then put it back up."

"Are you kidding me?"

"There is no other way, and it would be doing Kristy a favor. We'll put the wall back up, and make the doorway wider."

"Jesus Christ. Well, text her then, and make sure it's okay."

We get her permission to move forward.

"You know this issue is exactly why she gave this piano to you, right?" I don't answer. It's a gift from a friend; I don't care why she gave it to me.

Billy stomps to his truck and retrieves two crowbars and two hammers. We carefully pry off the wallboards, one by

42

one, and save them for replacement. Three hours later, my adrenaline continues to race, and I'm aching to get our new piano to its forever home.

Adopting is never easy, regardless of whether it's a pet, a baby, or for me, this piano. I would never tell a child that caring for them is too hard. I would never give up a pet because they misbehave due to a history of neglect or abuse. I won't give up on this piano.

The tenant returns. Right away, he begins offering instructions on how to handle our situation. Billy continues to work and I can see him huffing away words he would like to say in return. Billy's eyes meet mine, and I read his meaning. He's thinking, "I fucking told you so. I knew this would turn into a whole day's project, and if that tenant doesn't shut the hell up, I'm going to punch him."

"Thank you, honey," I say. "This means a lot to me."

"I know it does. I'm trying my best." Sweat drips down his forehead. His shirt has darkened under his armpits and at the small of his back. We skip lunch.

Even with the deconstructed wall now out of the way, the immense weight of the piano makes it difficult for one man and one woman to move it. By the time we find the exact angle for the piano to fit out of the newly enlarged living room exit, it's completed a three-hundred-point turn. Another hour has passed. Together we push her out of the living room. The wheels of the dollies bounce over the doorjamb.

Billy wraps appliance straps under the circumference of the piano and also around his wrists. He bends into a squat.

His thick legs and muscular chest constrict under the weight of the piano. His strength impresses me, and I'm attracted to his burly figure and perfect posture. Billy is the only man I have ever known with the physical and mental strength of a warrior while still having the ability to remain vulnerable and intimate. It's one of the many beautiful things about him.

He instructs me to push when he lifts. I do. The piano moves an inch onto the wooden platform that Billy constructed to bridge the gap between the house, the cement steps, and the trailer. It's official—we are moving the piano.

Dark clouds begin to form in the sky. "Billy, is it supposed to rain?"

"I don't think so."

The wind picks up. Moisture saturates the air as a thunderstorm boils its way toward us. I begin to panic. "It's going to rain. Oh no. What are we going to do?"

"Focus, Tina. It's not going to rain. Ready? Push." He lifts—another inch. Repeat.

We get her onto the wooden bridge. She sways back and forth like a giant tractor-trailer that has taken a corner too fast and is now trying to regain control. I try to hold her upright. My one hundred and thirty pounds of body weight doesn't impact the piano's rocking. I'm terrified, as if my child is in danger of being injured. When I feel out of control and helpless, I either flee or fight. The worst feeling I can think of as a mother is not being there for my child when she needs me. Right now, this piano is scaring the hell out of me, and I'm fighting like a protective mother to keep her from harm.

Billy wraps his arms around one side of the piano and stabilizes her movement. "Okay, hold her steady to keep her from falling over, and I'll push," he says. I'm standing at ground level, below the piano as it teeters on a wooden platform that could buckle under its weight at any moment. I know that if the piano wanted to fall on me, it would, and I would be dead. Maybe that fear is what gives me the strength to support her just as Billy instructed, because after one more hour has passed, we have finally inched her onto the trailer.

I jump for joy and scream, "Yahoo! We did it." I feel the cold tickle of droplets from the sky on my face. "Oh no. Billy, it's starting to rain, and we don't have any tarps." The one worst-case scenario we did not consider—rain.

"Get the blankets you brought and wrap it up." We kick into high gear and move as fast as our exhausted bodies are able. I wrap the piano with the blankets and use duct tape to secure them around it while he rebuilds the wall inside the house.

Another hour has passed by the time Billy finishes the wall. The rain has thankfully remained sparse and light, and so far, the piano is still dry. He returns to the truck to secure the blanket-covered piano so it's standing upright against the back of the trailer. Before he's done, the sky blackens and begins dropping buckets of rain on us. Mud splatters up onto the truck and the sides of the trailer as the rain impacts the ground.

Billy rushes to finalize the straps, using all of our bungee cords, "just in case." The piano's weight worries us, and we're unsure if the straps are strong enough to keep her from falling over on the bumpy ride home.

We load the gold carpet, now even heavier from the rain, onto the trailer, hoping it will cushion the piano should it fall, knowing we will have to pay to dispose of the rug at the dump later.

"Another freebie for Kristy," says Billy.

"Stop it, honey. Getting rid of that disgusting carpet is the least we can do. Kristy gave us this piano for free."

"Do you call that free?"

I touch his knuckles. "Thank you."

We pull out of the driveway, attempting a slow and steady exit. The air blurs with rain, and we are soaked. So much water is hitting the ground at once, and with nowhere to go, it streams down the center of the pavement.

I click the seatbelt around my chest, keeping it loose enough that I can turn around. I shift my body in my seat to face backward and watch our newborn baby behind us in the trailer. Tears empty down my cheeks. I want to protect her from the cruel world outside. I want to keep her safe and dry, but there is nothing I can do. I fear the blankets aren't enough to keep the rain from ruining her, but I also won't let Billy drive over twenty-five miles per hour. And with every bump, railroad track, or tailgating motorist, I squeal for him to slow down.

He's patient with me. Somehow he knows that I need him to be patient just as much as I need this piano. He reaches out to take my quivering hand and says, "It will be okay, honey."

I am not sure of that. Worry presses my eyebrows together, and my breathing is quick and irritated. I squeeze Billy's hand—harder every time I see her sway against the straps. The blankets, soaked in seconds, suck onto her frame like clothes do after you go swimming in them.

All of what we just went through was a high enough price to obtain such a beauty. Why must it rain too? And not just a sprinkle but a rain so heavy it makes cars pull over because they can't see. Rain that washes houses away in landslides and floods out roads and basements.

The sound of the rain pounding the roof of the truck hypnotizes me into a sea of tears. I imagine my tears are rain, and they are soaking this piano with all that I have been through in this life. The rain becomes necessary; otherwise, my fear will overwhelm me. I imagine it's washing away the piano's past, baptizing her into my arms and our home. The rain is a collection of my tears, the times when my eyes were cried out and dry with unnerving sadness and fear. I will move forward, I think. This voyage will come to an end once she is home safe.

The massive weight of the piano becomes the unmovable moments that seared themselves into my mind. Moments this piano will take away for me. Music will lift the heft of their burdens, and in return, I will adopt this musical heirloom to my home. My home will become filled with gratitude for its presence. She will not be left behind if we move, she will not be turned over to a new family or put up for adoption.

The gravity of the piano's purpose in my life is much too

substantial to consider her a temporary fixture. This piano is the newest member of our family, and even if I don't play, even if her keys end up ignored, I will no longer allow the sounds of a broken home to inflict fear and panic into my adult self.

When we arrive home, Billy backs the trailer into the garage. The piano is out of the rain. Ashlynn meets us inside the garage. We unwrap the restraints securing the piano and peel away the wet blankets. Its dark color has been changed white—its body has become one giant water stain.

"Oh no," I say.

Ashlynn caresses the piano. "I bet it will go away when it's dry, Mamma."

I smile at Ashlynn. "I bet you're right, sweet girl."

And she was.

Chapter Four

Beach Day

Summer in Maine is precisely how life should be. And the perfect place to enjoy it is at a beach. Today, Ashlynn and I have planned one of our favorite kinds of days—sunbathing and picnicking at Willard Beach followed by antiquing all the way home.

I'm heading into my twenty-ninth year, working full-time in the field of dentistry. Weekends are precious. They allow me to recover from the strain of taking care of other people's needs during the week. Ashlynn loves the sunshine and any opportunity for unique social media photos and videos. Willard Beach will satisfy us both.

We drive through the familiar streets of South Portland, and I point out (for the one-hundredth time) my middle school, my high school, the road I used to live on, Sam DePetrio's Market—where we stop to pick up Italian sandwiches for our picnic—and Willard Square. The sun is bright, and the open window allows the warm wind to blow Ashlynn's beautiful long brown hair away from her face. She gives me a sweet smile and says, "I know, Mamma," in response to every repeated exclamations.

We approach the four-way stop at the top of the cross-roads of Chase Street—where I lived the most consecutive years of my childhood—and Sawyer Street. I see a man who appears out of place. He's wearing dark jeans, work boots, and a heavy sweatshirt with the hood covering the back of his head. He strolls along the roadside in the heat of the day, as if he has nowhere in particular to go. He exhales a white puff of cigarette smoke. As we pass him, I stare at his face. He removes his hood and returns my glare.

The older, wiser part of me dismisses him as a man dressed for manual labor. Perhaps he's a landscaper, a builder, or maybe working on his own home. After all, Billy dresses similarly if his task requires it of him, even in the heat of summer.

The scared child inside me thinks of John Grant, the man who tried to kill my father more than once. The man I have been scared to death of my whole life.

———

I don't remember when he shot my father—I simply cannot recall the incident. It's possible that I don't know because I was so young, or maybe because it was too scary. My mother told me that in a bar, Getty's Pub in Bar Harbor, John Grant shot my father in the gut. My father, who was in the middle of whatever dispute was happening, came between the gun and a police officer. Heroism maybe?

According to my mother, his hospital stay was intensive, and the waiting room had a constant rotation of women—his many girlfriends. "The waiting room was full of women who claimed they were his wife so they could see him. I'm his goddamned wife," my mother would always say when telling the story. Since they got married when she was fifteen years old and pregnant with me, and they divorced only three years later, she was maybe sixteen or seventeen when he got shot. He was twenty-one.

His infidelity was a recurring explosive offense in the development of my lack of trust in men. Or maybe the source of my confusion was that my mother could not keep their issues between the two of them. I blame them both, but I learned many things at much too young an age to ever develop an opinion of the world as a safe and loving place. Again, bragging rights to trauma earned, which is what defined my mother.

I do remember his scar—a foot-long incision that crossed the length of his abdomen. His newest battle wound shown off with pride, as he was often topless—just another tattoo of the complex life of Tarzan. No wonder everyone knew his name. He was the town's handsome bad boy who took a bullet from John Grant and sent him to jail for it.

It was when John Grant got out of jail that I became even more terrified. He had a debt to settle with my father. Alcohol and hot-headedness are never a good combination. My father earned his nickname, Tarzan, for not being the most levelheaded and stable man from Southwest Harbor. He and his family could be the sole reason residents stayed away from the other side of the island back then.

John Grant almost succeeded the second time he tried killing my father. If he hadn't mistaken one of my father's friends for him that night, he might have.

———

This memory envelopes me as heat blurs the air above the pavement in front of us. The habitual drive toward Willard Beach is so familiar, I barely need to pay attention. Without realizing it, my foot has almost come off the accelerator, and our car is hardly moving. A motorist behind us honks.

"Oh, sorry. I wasn't paying attention," I say to Ashlynn.

"Jerk," Ashlynn mouths to the passing car.

Most times, I feel my memories from start to finish. Like reading a book from cover to cover. I see where the moment begins and travel through the images, smells, and emotions to completion. I would see snapshots of a particular moment if it had a climax—a visual record made of vinyl, skipping on repeat.

Remembering is feeling. This memory is a book. It's one incident that tells a million things with a single image. During the last mile of driving with my daughter to our favorite beach, my mind goes elsewhere.

———

I am under the covers. No man is in the house tonight, so I'm playing the part of my mother's bedmate. Casey is alone in his bed down the hall. There are no lights on in the trailer, but moonlight reveals every inch of her bedroom. It was one of those precious-to-me nights when my mom and I talked and giggled ourselves far from sleep.

A loud crash outside stuns us into muteness. It was an abnormal noise that boomed through the silence outside, unlike any sound my young self had ever heard. I stand on my mother's bed to look out of the window. There is nothing but blackness. Silence resumes, so we ignore it and settle back into bed.

A few moments later, we hear car tires skidding into our dirt driveway. A man's voice, panicked and nightmarish, pierces the night. We hear one door slam, then another. We run to the front door. My father thrusts the door open and stumbles in with his arm wrapped around an unconscious man—his friend Terry.

Blood covers them. The terror in my father's face induces panic within me. His cheeks shine with sweat, and one of his eyes is swollen. His beard and mustache appear wet. His light brown hair, soft and naturally curly, is plastered to his forehead with sweat. Intoxication pulls his eyebrows down, narrowing my view of his green eyes.

A half-circle of flesh hangs from Terry's scalp, and his thinning hair has become matted with a thick mixture of dried and fresh blood. His skin is whiter than usual, and his lips appear blueish.

"John Grant is chasing us. He hit a telephone pole on the Crooked Road. Then he beat the shit out of Terry with a baseball bat." Terry is motionless.

"That must have been the noise we heard," my mother says

as Casey tiptoes toward us. He squeezes between my mother and me, taking in the scene with wide and terrified eyes.

"We need an ambulance for Terry. He's in bad shape." My father lays him on our brown-and-orange plaid couch.

My mother calls for an ambulance. Casey and I huddle close to each other, listening to my father's account of the evening. He taps his pack of cigarettes on the kitchen table and pulls one from the box. He snaps a match from a book and lights the cigarette, the sound of it catching fire sizzles through the cold air. I find this predictable act of him and his cigarette comforting—a spot of normalcy amid the horror of a shattered man's skull and a cataclysmic disruption to our quiet night.

My father's movements are regular. He sits at the table in his usual place. He crosses one leg over the other and leans back in the chair like he always does. Watching him settles my stomach. His bicep bulges against his forearm every time he bends his hand in for a drag off his cigarette. His round knuckles and strong hands hold the white tobacco-filled cylinder with tenderness. His skin is brown from working outside in the sun. His green eyes and handsome face go from smiling to worried as he retells the incident.

"Terry and I were at Geddy's, and all hell broke loose when John Grant walked in. We got thrown out of the bar for starting a brawl. John Grant chased us on foot, then chased us by car from Bar Harbor to Hulls Cove." I look at my father's feet. He's wearing his black square-toed leather boots tucked under his blue jeans. Another predictable sight. I exhale.

"Jesus, we were all over the road. Lucky for us, John Grant hit a telephone pole. It fell and blocked the road, so he couldn't chase us. We figured he was hurt. So we got out to check. But John Grant had a baseball bat and wanted to fight. All of us were drunk and not seeing straight. He thought Terry was me." My father coughs out a laugh, and white bursts of smoke exit his mouth.

John Grant thought Terry was Tarzan and took the bat to him first. My father got John Grant away from Terry but not without taking the bat to his skull too.

"I punched him pretty hard a few times." My father stretches out the thick fingers of his right hand. His knuckles are swollen and bleeding. "I got Terry back in the car and escaped."

It must have been close. We heard the crash, I thought.

"Tina, get a blanket," orders my mother. All I can find is a sleeping bag. My mother pulls the zipper to open the sleeping bag and covers Terry's body with it. Blood streams down the side of his head. "Casey, sit here and keep an eye on him." Our mother pulls the round leather ottoman adjacent to Terry's face. Casey sits down. He leans toward Terry, holding his elbows in his hands. "Let us know if he stops breathing." I remember my brother and I shared the task. We were silent, scared to death, and both under age seven.

The ambulance does not come. Time stands still. I listen for noises—anything that might sound like John Grant outside—while my parents sit at the kitchen table. They rehash the events of the evening over and over again. My father holds a towel to his head, and his elbows rest on his knees. Their chain-smoking fills the trailer with clouds of uncertainty. My brother and I shiver in the chill of the trailer's living room, watching over a man who could have been dead for all we knew.

My mother calls for the ambulance again. "The telephone pole is blocking them," she says. "They have to go around. It will be another fifteen minutes, at least."

———

I don't recall the arrival of the ambulance; however, I remember the very next day, when my mother showed my brother and me where it happened. We sit at the stop sign at the end of our dirt road. My mother waits for a passing car. I peer out the window at Blanche's house. My brother and I found a batch of kittens on her land. She came to pick them up roaring complaints at us and stuffing the kittens into a netted bag which she planned to use to drown them all. Casey and I cried and begged for our mother to make her stop. Our mother did nothing. We visited the site where we discovered the kittens and found one more. She was blind in one eye and very young. We rescued her and named her Kitty.

We exited our road, Old Norway Drive, and turned right onto the Crooked Road. After we cleared the immediate small hill, we spotted the downed pole, now pushed out of the road. It was less than a quarter of a mile from our trailer.

"Oh my God, it was so close to home. Jesus Christ. What if he knows where we live?" my mother said when she saw it.

The staples in my father's and Terry's heads were numerous, and the smell of their hospital stays forever trapped in my memory bank. Terry's life was touch-and-go for days. He did recover, though. The next time I saw him, he passed out drunk at our kitchen table and fell to the floor, landing in Kitty's food. We all laughed at him and left him there. My mother took a photo.

I chuckle out loud at this thought. Ashlynn looks at me with a smile. "What?"

"Nothing, honey, I just had a random thought. I'm excited for the beach." Ashlynn resumes singing along with the song on the radio.

———

I'm sure my mother was terrified. This had happened in the '70s, when she was still a child herself. She lacked the protection of a father, which she needed and deserved; however, she was a mother at the same time. Not that her father was absent. He was there, put food on their table, and yelled at everyone.

My mother was starved for love and sought it out in the only way she knew how—tormented, toxic, and under the influence of whatever drug drove the intensity up. She never found the love she was looking for. And she never learned to have compassion for herself.

She hated everything about herself—her decisions, her appearance, her thoughts—no part of her was ever good enough or correct in her eyes.

———

I inhale the smell of our Italian sandwiches that we picked up at Sam DePetrio's market. Hunger pulls at my stomach. I anticipate the calmness the scent and sounds of the ocean will provide. I yearn to leave behind this restless feeling and the memory of fear inspired by the man who tried to kill my father.

As we near the parking lot at Willard Beach, I cannot help remembering when my mother moved us to this town. No matter how far away we were, John Grant haunted us.

———

Again, my mother moved us away from Bar Harbor. I was in fifth grade by that time, and my brother was in fourth grade, just a year and a half younger than me. "We have to get away from your father's reputation," our mother would say over and over again.

For the first time, I had found something I loved: swimming. I had joined the Sharks Swim Team in Bar Harbor and was improving with rapid leaps and bounds. As I write this now, I realize that my love for swimming developed because I had overcome a great fear—the water—a fear I developed after my grandfather got lost at sea, even though he didn't care how scared I was of it possibly happening to me. Being on the swim team gave me control of something. Swimming gave me power and independence. My coach, Lenny—the first of many—was firm and attentive.

Regardless, we packed up our car and drove to Portland, Maine. To be exact, we went to her new job at Martins Point on Veranda Street. The parking lot was empty. We sat in the car and waited. And waited. No one came. We had no place to go—no apartment, no friend's house to stay in, no plan. We were homeless.

My mother eventually decided to leave the safety of the car. She led us to the nearest house—a stranger's home—and knocked on the door. "Can I use your phone?" she asked. A woman, draping her arm around the shoulders of her teenage son, let us in. My mother called the man who had hired her. While they discussed our predicament, I scanned the house. I felt like I was from another world and had just stepped into an alternate reality.

My brother and I huddled our small frames close to our mother's legs and under the wall-mounted telephone. I remember longing for the comfort of a home like that. The television sent flashes of alternating lights through the darkened spacious living room. The couch, filled with fat pillows, was covered in blankets that had been tossed haphazardly across its back, giving it an appeal of comfort on that particular Saturday afternoon. An empty glass sat next to a dish sprinkled with crumbs on the book cluttered coffee table, and pair of white socks with dirtied bottoms draped over an arm of the sofa. Art in beautiful frames decorated the walls and the air was void of stale cigarettes.

Somehow, my mother landed us a temporary apartment—one that her new employer reserved for the doctors at

Martin's Point on Veranda Street. The generosity of her new boss saved us from being homeless. Or perhaps, I assumed, he'd only helped us because he too wanted to have sex with her. Right, Mom?

Our mother began her new job working on computers— her self-taught talent—the following Monday morning.

For months my mother circled apartments for rent in the newspaper with a red pen, we visited many, and my brother and I went to a new scary school. Most apartments were much too expensive for us. She finally found one in our price range in South Portland, on Chase Street—the first floor of a three-unit apartment house on the corner of the cutest neighborhood I'd ever seen. It was the most perfect place we had ever shared. That apartment was exactly what I had been waiting for my mother to find. We would be safe. I decided it was all worth the wait.

My sense of safety was short-lived. After only one week of life in our newest home and school under our belts, my mother had a John Grant sighting. She rushed into the apartment, stomping her feet, wide-eyed and breathing heavily. Her voice was panicked as she said, "I think I just saw John Grant. He was walking toward Sawyer Street. He told Tarzan he would get his family." Then she lifted the phone to call my father.

I remember sinking into the couch situated in front of a large window overlooking Chase Street and knowing we would never be safe. I imagined a black-haired man with wide eyebrows, a heavy beard, and chillingly angry features.

I still have no idea what he looked like and I never dared to ask. I always assumed he was taller and bigger than my father. After all, my father was feared by many due to his imposing stature as much as his reputation. Who could hurt him? If John Grant could scare my father, he must have been a monster.

Here I was experiencing another moment when I was bursting with fear but had no choice but to go on with life as if nothing out of the ordinary was happening. It was our ordinary.

I found a swim team. I rode my bicycle to practice at five a.m. every day that summer, then back to school for track in the afternoon. During the school year, my friend's mother drove us to swim practice. Without them, I would have had to walk the five miles to swim practice, often in the snow. Sometimes I'd jog home if I was feeling fat and thought I needed the extra exercise.

"Tina, have you ever seen a video of someone running in slow motion? It bounces your skin and will make it sag. You'll start to look old if you keep running," my mother often informed me. But how was I supposed to make her happy by being skinny?

———

Ashlynn and I pull into the parking lot of Willard Beach. We are early enough that we secure an elusive parking spot. I turn off the car's engine, and heat immediately envelopes us. I focus on the sounds around us—I breathe in a mixture of beach-rose, sunblock, and ocean. I exhale and release my fear of John Grant. I focus on my love for Ashlynn. She pushes her mirrored sunglasses up her nose and slings her beach bag over her shoulder.

"I love the beach, Mamma."

"I do too, honey. It just feels so good."

Chapter Five

The Settee

Ashlynn and I spread out our purple butterfly-patterned blanket-size towel on the sand. The air is still and the sun is hot. The sounds of gentle rushing waves and children's voices draw pleasure within my core. We paint our bodies with sunblock and settle in to eat our lunch first. Seagulls and sand fleas try to join in on the feast.

Soon we are both meditating as we lie on our backs, cradled between the soft sand and the warm sky. I peek at my daughter from under my straw hat that's protecting my face from the damaging sun. She appears to be asleep. I'm happy she's feeling so restful. It's rare for us to get beach time together, maybe once a summer since she began high school, but so precious to us both.

I settle my hat back over my face and close my eyes. My thoughts wander to millions of destinations every day, but it's inevitable that they always find their way to my childhood. The familiar sense of fear I conjured from my memories of John Grant still lingers under my breath. The next thing I recall is my father's hospitalization due to alcohol poisoning.

Beyond a normal rehab program, he was hospitalized during his recovery. Maybe he almost died, or it was an attempt to avoid more jail time.

———

The rehab program at Bangor Hospital was forceful. I'm sure the program was based on the scientific knowledge of the time, or perhaps experience had proven it to be effective, but it was harsh for our family. Traumatic, to say the least. In my opinion, it was almost as traumatic as living with an alcoholic. I still haven't recovered from this experience, and I dare say my brother has not either.

I recall Christmas Eve that year in my father's hospital room during his rehab stay, where my mother brought my brother and me each a present to open. Mine—training bras. I was as flat as a two-by-four, but my mother, trying to be motherly, wanted my ill-connecting father to be fatherly. He whistled a catcall. I didn't even smile.

It reminded me of when he would visit the trailer between drinking benders that had lasted days or weeks. I would be excited to see him, but all he would do was sit at the table with my mother, smoke cigarettes, and drink coffee. To feel included, I would play waitress. He'd flirt with me in same the way he flirted with other women that were not my mother. He would pinch my butt and ask, "What time do you get off?"

"Never," I would reply and stop playing. My answer always made my dad laugh. The whole thing made me frustrated. Both of my parents ignored me most of the time, but whenever they paid attention, they commented on my body while my mother complained about hers.

It was an hour's drive from Hulls Cove to Bangor, and we were about halfway to the hospital that Christmas Eve when our car broke down. I think my grandfather came to help us. Either that or Casey and I went to the side of the road to flag down a stranger for help—our cars broke down so often that I'm not sure who ended up helping us that night.

My brother and I received promises of a late Christmas celebration, after Dad was out of the hospital. My birthday was four days after Christmas too. Neither happened that year. Instead, we were given the gift of torture through rehab at the hospital.

————

The coconut scent of sunblock reminds me how far from that Christmas I am. Thank God. The sun's heat on my skin calms me to the point of almost falling asleep. But instead, I think about rehab Christmas.

————

Not only did my and my brother's developing minds learn about the roles family members of an alcoholic adopt for survival, but we were diagnosed into our prospective roles by the staff. Parts that we would live out forever.

My brother, six years old at the time, was told he was "the mascot" and "the lost child." Based on those labels, he would provide comic relief to avoid feeling the pain. Additionally, they predicted he would self-medicate with chemicals, perpetuating the cycle of addiction. He was deemed likely to grow into an adult addict who wouldn't seek attention or love, would have difficulty forming relationships, and would finally isolate himself as a way to cope.

You could say he either followed their instructions, or they had a crystal ball. But I think they're responsible for forming a traumatized six-year-old's opinion of himself. Now, at age forty-seven, he has lived the exact addict-induced life path suggested to him at age six.

They labeled me "the hero." Sounds great at first, but I, too, am doomed for failure. You see, the counselors told me that the family hero is your typical Type A personality: a hard-working, overachieving perfectionist. The hero tries to bring the family together and create a sense of normalcy with achievements. The hero is often the eldest child, as they seek to give hope to the rest of the family. However, the driving force behind the family hero puts an extreme amount of pressure on her. She is seeded to crack at some point. Adult heroes of addicted families have high anxiety and are susceptible to stress-related illnesses.

I may have been the family hero in my addiction-riddled hell, but I will not fail. I will not allow my parents' bullshit to define me, nor the assessments of the staff who—with or without intentions of doing so—set forth the personal destinies of myself and my brother. If I could advise them now, I would say, "Keep that shit to adults only. Do not share demoralizing words with children when we are in desperate need of some wind beneath our wings."

The counselors diagnosed my mother as "the enabler." I think she was also an addict and the family scapegoat. She allowed it, participated in it, and often blamed herself. It was all she knew how to do.

Establishing this type of family culture around an addict breeds addiction, disloyalty, pain, abuse, neglect, and, worst of all, the bottomless void of unhappiness. If the focus had been on breaking these roles instead of fitting us into them, maybe that's what would have prevailed.

The long call of a seagull brings me back to the beach. I remain mindful of this place in time and the happiness that being a mother brings me. The love I feel for my daughter makes me proud. I am a different person from my parents. I refer to the experiences recorded within my mind of their poor judgment and behavior as an example of what I don't want to emulate.

Trauma is carried on when the story of it is shared with someone not old enough to hear it. Sharing instead of or without healing passes the trauma from generation to generation: the legacy of trauma that will ensure familial devastation.

Today at the beach, although my mind is heavy with the past, I keep these memories to myself. They are not Ashlynn's burden, and I am strong enough to carry their heavy weight on my own. I smile under my straw hat. I'm proud of myself for this. Sharing how traumatic my father's rehab stay was for me will not help Ashlynn in any way—but teaching her to say no to drugs will.

———

During my father's sobriety-focused hospital stay, the rehab staff brought us to a large room. Dad sat alone in the middle. My mother, brother, and I sat on the cold metal chairs that were facing him. Other addicted inmates and their families surrounded us. It was called the circle.

The day before, counselors guided us through a writing exercise. They told us to write Dad a letter and a list of the awful things he had done so we could read it to him at the circle. This letter would allow him to see that he needed to stop drinking. Someone helped my brother write his. As I tried to write mine, I remember having nothing to say.

How can a seven-year-old articulate, let alone write, about these experiences? I did not know how to express my worries. Nor did I have the ability to weed through what was standard parent behavior versus not. I'd had zero normal life events or relationships for comparison purposes. This was our normal, and I had zero experience living any other way. I knew I felt awful. My sadness was so heavy, I swore I weighed two hundred pounds. I had the instinctual needs for love and safety, but my parents never met those needs. I was lonely and angry, and I bullied my friends because of it.

I was so jealous of this one girl in my grade, Heather, whose mother packed her a perfect lunch in an orange Tupperware lunch box set every day for school. I belittled her, embarrassed her, and punched her in the face, knocking out a baby tooth. She must have been so happy when we moved to Portland. With the genius of Facebook, I found her online in 2016 and apologized for the hell I put her through.

I didn't know how to deal with or describe the pain I was feeling. I was too afraid. I was scared to hurt my father. And they wanted me to write about the bad things he did? The man who I would do anything to make smile, even though I wasn't even sure if he loved me. How could I tell him he was awful?

I know he hurt my mother. He cheated on her, yelled at her, made her cry. She cheated on him, yelled at him, then she would cry. When he was around, it was about my mother, or him, not me. My relationship with him was based on his relationship with my mother. We did not have a relationship separate from her. I knew his primary loves in life were cigarettes, women, and motorcycles. Not me. My mother's loves in life were any kind of love she could get from a man—again, not me.

Why couldn't I tell him about the writing award I got in first grade? How my teacher scared me because she grabbed my arm and pulled me down the hallway like I was in trouble. She stopped pulling me and turned me to face the wall. There, on the wall, hung my story with a blue, first-place ribbon on it. My teacher smiled at me but didn't say a word. She held my shoulders and stood behind me while we both ignored the busy hallway and stared at my paper.

The award winning story was about my dad and me ice skating in the Olympics. The crowd cheered for us. We were both so happy, and our routine was flawless. Then the story ended with the reality that it was only a dream. It was the only writing award I ever received and the only positive acknowledgment I ever got from any of my teachers.

Most of my teachers knew my mom. Some even called me Diane. Hell, it hadn't been very long since she was a student in their classrooms.

Or maybe we could talk about Casey falling off the jungle gym and landing on his face. The impact packed dirt under his eyelids, and he was bleeding from his nose and mouth. An ambulance took him to the hospital, and I was left at school to worry. But rehab was not about Casey or me. Rehab was about him. They never mentioned the role of the tormented witnesses and how no one ever talked about us.

———

I lay here with my eyes closed, soaking in the sun's love on the beach with the love of my life, Ashlynn. I realize that even now, at age forty-nine, I am still learning how to write about the awful things my parents did and the dreadful things their parents did to them. Things like my mother's rape at age eleven, or my father witnessing the repeated sexual abuse of his sister by his father, or the belief that his father killed his mother out of jealousy. Or about how my father burned down his own father's house. And then there was the crazy man who wanted to kill us.

A mother and her young son shuffle past us. The sand the boy is pushing with each step splashes my feet with needle-like pricks on my skin. I chuckle in silence.

———

So, since I had nothing to say in the circle on that day, almost forty-two years ago, I wrote what I heard in the classes my mother forced me to attend: I was afraid he would die. I never knew if he was coming back. When he was drunk, I was scared. As I read the words that weren't mine, as mild as they were, I was so afraid. I cried, and he cried. My heart broke, and it has never healed. I can still reproduce the pain I felt that day when I dwell on the moment. It has not faded with time.

There was so much more to fix than just my father's drinking.

———

"Mamma?" murmurs Ashlynn.

"Yeah, honey. I'm awake."

"I'm getting too hot. I'm ready to leave whenever you are."

"Okay, sweetie, I'm ready. We can go now." I sit up and look at her. "Are you feeling okay?"

"Yeah, but my blood sugar feels a little low."

"I'll peel you an orange before we pack up. That'll fix it."

I remove one of the two oranges from our cooler. I stick my thumb into it and remove its thick shell. She eats the orange fast and takes long, deep breaths.

"It's already working," she says.

"Oranges work the fastest, honey. That's why I always pack them."

She smiles. We shake off the blankets and fold them into our beach bag. Ashlynn carries the cooler, and I take the bags.

The car is hot, and the black leather seats sear our skin. We lay towels down and try to sit again. "Ashlynn, do you feel better? Are you up to stopping at Cherished Possessions?"

"Yes, absolutely, I'm looking forward to it."

Cherished Possessions is an antique consignment shop we visit every time we go to Willard Beach together. We love scanning through the rotation of items put up for sale and always seem to find something we adore. The prices reduce the longer something remains unsold—a clever way to keep the merchandise moving.

The car's air-conditioning has just cooled enough to chill our hot skin when we arrive at Cherished Possessions. We park in the lot behind the store, and as we walk toward the entrance, we brush off the dried sand still sticking to our ankles. The door is ajar, held open with a bright yellow lobster buoy.

There is no air-conditioning inside. The warm air feels heavy—thick with aged aromas. There are two others in the store, an older couple who I assume are husband and wife. They shuffle along between the displays, staying ahead of us.

My time shopping with Ashlynn procures an extroverted joy within me—the opposite of my usual introverted solitary shopping. I enjoy chit-chatting with her and the store clerks, and I find myself asking questions and instigating conversations. She delights me with her curiosity and affinity for small, cute things—tiny tins, ceramic animals, brooches, teacups, and old letters.

"Mom, isn't this so cute?" She holds up a miniature ceramic tea set that's barely large enough to use with a baby doll. I kiss her forehead. She has so much little girl inside of her still. Ashlynn pretends to sip from the aged, petite cup as her long, elegant fingers pinch the handle, holding it to her lips. It strikes me so funny, like a giant from *Alice in Wonderland*. This child-woman of mine, so statuesque and refined, playing pretend with a tea set.

I blurt out a boisterous laugh. "Shhhh," Ashlynn says and laughs just as hard as I do. We receive annoyed glances from the other two shoppers ahead of us. We plop ourselves into the nearest couch and giggle ourselves to painful stomachs. She repeats the act that was so random yet so hysterical, and she rejoices in my happiness.

At long last, we regain control of ourselves. I take notice of the settee where we have made ourselves at home. I place my hands on its fabric and caress the pale-yellow rose pattern with my palm. Ashlynn pays attention, as always. "Oh, Mom, this is so pretty."

"Isn't it?"

Our love and laughter become collected into this object,

and I become attached to this moment, on this couch, shopping for antiques—a place where we have shared such glee. A feeling I ached for the day we moved to Portland. The day I stood huddled with my brother in a stranger's house, longing for the comfort of their couch.

"I think I want to buy it. I wonder if we can fit it in the car?"

"If we lay the seats down, I bet it will." Ashlynn's eyes are a window to her soul. I can read poetry pouring from her insides. Heartbreaking when I see that she's feeling pain, but right now, I see joy. I feel joy. Her green eyes are clear and beautiful. Her long, naturally curly hair is tangled and full of volume from the ocean breeze. She has it piled on top of her head with an orange scrunchy that matches her bikini. We share the most beautiful moments, and I want her to remember them.

"Ashlynn, take that end, I'll take this end, and we'll move her to the register and then continue looking around. I just don't want someone else to take it."

"Okay, Mamma."

We move the love seat to the front. "We want this settee, but we're still shopping. Is it okay to leave it here?" I ask.

"Absolutely. Isn't this a beautiful couch? It arrived last week. Someone was supposed to pick it up this morning, but they never showed."

"Lucky for me." I caress the hand-carved wood that crowns the backrest with an elegant slope toward the armrest. I find myself attracted to its beauty, as if I recognize it as a missing part of me. Once I obtain it, that part of me will be whole. One of the trillions of moments unsettled in my memory quieted and new.

Ashlynn finds a normal-sized teacup decorated with red and pink roses along with a matching saucer. "Can I get this, Mamma? I want to plant a succulent in it."

"Oh, what a great idea. Yes, of course." She finds two more with different designs and colors for her collection.

We complete an entire expedition of the ancient collage of artifacts and finish our exploring at the register. We pay for the teacups and the settee. I fold the back seats forward, and Ashlynn helps me slide the couch into the hatchback of the car. It fits with two inches to spare.

As we drive home, we make a stop at Skillin's Greenhouse for three succulents. I can't resist the flourishing annuals with bright flowers, so I pick up a few more for the back deck.

We introduce the couch to her new forever home and situate her in the sunny reading room. Our cats rub against her legs, and the dogs collect a complete inventory of smells before accepting the new couch as part of the pack. Ashlynn works under the sunshine on the deck as she transfers the succulents to the teacups. I insert the flowering annuals into a large clay pot, drench them with water, then rest my back against the side of the house.

The faraway hum of cars moving along the interstate purrs in the background. An occasional moan of tires on the rumble strip is the only reminder that the sound is even there. Content panting from our two dogs and music from the birds evoke blissfulness within me. This day, this moment, this life—I am living away from the self-inflicted trap of not knowing better. I escaped. Though not without the plague of traumatic injury, which I will forever be a carrier. I made a conscious choice to be different and find beauty in my past within pieces of history, like our new settee.

I am happy to be alive and that my mother did not give us up for adoption. Instead, she chose to be a mother—responsible for showing us the world, her world. She was not wise with age and experience, nor was she loving, patient, or selfless. She was an abused, neglected mother, a child herself. She was desperate to find love, having survived a brutal home riddled with anger and addiction but not without injury. Her real-life nightmare took center stage in my and my brother's developing minds. But she tried, and she did it alone.

As ill-equipped a mother as she was, I loved her and still do. I adore my father and always have. As absent and ignorant as he was, he was a fierce survivor of worse than I could ever imagine. Because of their lives and mine, I know I'm suited to succeed at overcoming whatever obstacles may threaten my path. The mundane struggles of everyday life are a weak comparison to the trials of the past. And though the recording of my life replays at whim and often without my control, it remains internal. I have vowed not to live in the horrors of my past, and therefore I am not passing on the trauma to the love of my life, my only daughter.

However, I worry. Am I too damaged to be better?

Chapter Six

The Birds and the Bees

Today is my dead mother's birthday. July 23. She would have been sixty-five. Ashlynn and I sit on the wood floor of our living room with stacks of photo albums around us. Ashlynn wants to post some photos of her Grammy-Di on Instagram to honor her birthday today.

She finds a full-face black-and-white picture of my mother—possibly the world's first selfie. She most likely took this photo of herself sometime between 1968 and '72. On the wall behind her is a poster of the real Tarzan cloaked in a leopard print loincloth. Around her wrist is a homemade beaded bracelet that reads *Diane*.

"Oh, look at this one, Mom," says Ashlynn. "There's a poster that says *Tarzan*."

"Ha. Oh my God, I never noticed that before. I always looked at the daisy in her hair and her bob haircut. Look how big her eyes are. That's where you get your eyes, sweetie, from your grammy." Ashlynn smiles.

"I'm going to scan this one." Ashlynn holds her phone over the photo and presses the exposure button for three seconds.

An app scans the image, tweaks the clarity and color, and saves a digital copy into her phone's photographs.

I find a picture of Mom and Dad sitting in front of a car with Corvair in chrome lettering across its hood. I, as a baby, sit between them. It would have been my first summer. "Can you scan this one, Ash?"

"Sure." She holds her phone over the image. "That's a cool car."

I smile at her comment as I recall my mother hating my birthday. "Can't we change your birthday to summer? It's so damn close to Christmas," she would say every single year. It was a strain financially for her—Christmas and my birthday just four days apart. I got toothpaste once.

The noiselessness of the photos strikes me. Internal sounds of these moments echo through my subconscious. Ashlynn paws through dozens of albums that have collected moments of my family history, but, in reality, they are false representations of the truth. They're snapshots of mere split seconds during events that were far from noiseless. A frozen tableau that appears normal. Our faces look fine. We smile in some and sit with our cousins in others. No one would ever know what our reality was. I examine my two-to three-year-old face—I can see worry, preoccupation, and fear.

Ashlynn only sees how cute I was.

———

Ashlynn was at her biological father's house when I discovered my mother was dead. My mother was a mere fifty-seven years old. I was forty-one.

It's a Saturday morning, and Billy and I are volunteering at the high school basketball concession stand when I receive a text from my brother that reads, *Mom's missing.*

What do you mean Mom's missing? I respond.

She was supposed to be here last night, and she never showed up.

I call him. "So you're just starting to look for Mom now?"

"Sometimes she goes to Gramp's first. Sandra is there, and they were waiting for her, too, but they thought she came to my house first."

"So she's not at Gramp's?"

"No. And, she's not answering her phone." My brother's voice was emotionless, still in a way that told me he was scared to death.

"Has anyone called the hospitals?"

"No."

"Okay, I'll go to her apartment. It's about twenty minutes from where I am right now, so I'll call the manager on my way over." We have always been able to find her if we needed to. Something was off.

I called her phone and left her a voice mail telling her she was freaking everyone out. Next, I called the condo manager. He said he would knock on her door and call me back. He never called back. I called him multiple times—no answer. Then a police officer answered the manager's phone.

"The chain lock is engaged from the inside of her condo, and your mother's car is still parked out front," said the female officer.

"Well, that means she's still inside. Cut the chain and go inside," I instruct.

"Okay, we just needed your permission," the officer says.

Billy and I arrive after the longest twenty-minute car ride of my life. He pulls our car into the nearest parking spot on High Street in Portland. I jump out while the vehicle is still moving and run down the sidewalk toward the front entrance of the Marlborough building. The constant force of the wind on High Street pushes against me and tries to slow my pace. I eye her car, still parked in front of her building. She never left.

I leap up the four flights of stairs, taking the steps two at a time to reach her floor. Four police officers shield the door, preventing me from entering her apartment. A grief counselor has already been called and is on-site, waiting for my arrival. I back away from them as they speak. "I'm sorry, but your mother passed away."

"What do you mean, passed away?" My back finds the opposing wall, and I sink to the floor. The grief counselor tries to be present for me. His nearness makes me want to punch him. I need space, air, and solitude. So I continue to push his hand from my shoulder. I cannot make eye contact with him or tolerate him in my personal space. Who is this person attempting to comfort me? Why the hell would I want comfort from a stranger when I couldn't even get it from the people I loved? I want to yell at him and tell him to go away, but like my fearful child self when my mother was having sex, I was frozen and could not speak up.

I had no idea how to show pain. My childhood had taught me that I needed to swallow physical and emotional pain. I needed to be strong. I couldn't yell "Ouch," or ask for help without being shamed. If I was sad, it was because I was feeling sorry for myself, not because of something external that was happening to me.

So, I say nothing.

Billy arrives after parking the car and asks the questions I am unable to voice.

"What happened? How did she die? Can Tina go in to see her?"

No one is telling us anything. No details. "We have to rule out foul play," is all they say. They won't let me into my mother's condominium until they have cleared the scene and ruled out homicide. A woman from a funeral home arrives at the request of the police. She informs me that my mother has died of natural causes and that they would be taking her out of the building soon and that I should not look.

"You are not taking her until I can see her," I say as boldly as I can from the floor.

"She is naked. It appears she just got out of the shower."

"Cover her up then. I have to see her." Do they want to protect me from seeing her naked? Jesus, it's way too late for that.

I've seen her naked more often than I've seen her clothed. My brother and I showered with her until seventh grade, and the only reason she stopped is that we outgrew the space.

"You kids are getting too big for this shit," she scolded. As if it was all our idea in the first place.

Directly after sex, she'd barge into the bathroom to remove her damn diaphragm—full of menstrual blood and semen—and dump the contents in the sink in front of me while I tried to pee. "When I'm on my period, I use my diaphragm so I can still have sex," she would explain. And some days, while trying to get ready for school, she would take over the sink, fill it with hot soapy water, drench a washcloth into the steaming water and scrub off the sex between her legs. "My vagina is two fingers wide. That's a normal size," she would add for no reason. Once she was finished, I would brush my teeth in the same sink.

"What do you mean by 'natural causes'? Does it mean she wasn't murdered?"

"Well, yes. We wanted to make sure no one else was involved in your mother's death."

"How did she die then?"

"We don't know exactly."

"But you know it's from natural causes? That tells me nothing. She was only fifty-seven. Natural causes for such a young woman are hard to believe. Shouldn't she have an autopsy?"

"You will have to pay for the autopsy yourself because the medical examiner has already ruled her death to be from natural causes."

"Fine."

The police officers cover her with a towel to make themselves feel better, then they allow me to see her. She has makeup on, and her hair is still wrapped in a towel. She's lying on her bed with her hands on her chest near her collarbone. She appears to be taking a nap.

Gravity has pooled her blood to the backside of her body. Her skin paled overnight, except for a deep purple line that runs the length of her head, neck, and shoulders that I can see—a stark contrast to the white comforter under her.

Her underwear drawer where she kept her vibrator is open. My eyes linger at the open drawer. I recall that, somehow, a few of my middle school and high school friends knew about her vibrator in the top drawer of her dresser, not hidden away under her underwear. They bragged about knowing such a scandalous secret. I conclude that she must have been masturbating when she died.

My mother masturbating when she died was not a shocking revelation for me. It is a fact. I'm sure of it. No one told me; I just knew. However forbidden the idea may be for others, I was not surprised that my mind went to this place with my mother. She was so open with her sexuality that not one thing I see or hear of others is shocking.

When we sold her condo and packed up her things, I never found her vibrator—this confirmed my theory.

Regardless, I got to see her before they took her body away. She looked peaceful and beautiful. Her painful life ended, but way too soon. Ashlynn's grammy—no, Ashlynn is too young to lose her. She needs her grammy for way longer than that.

The pathologist who performed my mother's autopsy phoned me with his findings less than a week later. She'd died of a stroke. A bleeding stroke. A subarachnoid hemorrhage stroke. He located the bleed sight at the base of her brain and blamed it on her years of smoking and alcohol consumption. He compared her vessels to an old, cracked, inflexible garden hose.

He inquired about my familial history of smoking-related illnesses. My maternal grandmother died at age sixty-two due to smoking-induced lung cancer, as did her brother. My paternal father died of a stroke while in the hospital for a smoking-induced lung issue in his forties. The pathologist asked about my cumulative amount of secondhand smoke— my entire childhood.

"Tell all of the women in your family not to smoke," he instructed.

I have never been a smoker. Regardless, I became riddled with panic, convinced that I only had sixteen years left to live. As I near ten years since then and only have six years left of this life, I am not sure I have convinced myself otherwise. However, having my mother out of my life has allowed me to have an inner awakening the likes of which I have never experienced.

I am free of the burden of her guilt-ridden expectations and black-and-white opinions of me. I know I am not the bitch she so often called me. I know sex is not my only power, and I know I am trustworthy and intelligent. I know my body and looks are not what I want to use to succeed in life, and I know I am a good mother. I know I want to love myself the way I am, but I'm not sure that's possible for me.

———

I raise my head toward Ashlynn. I watch her flip through the pages of a photo album from the '70s. There is no longer any adhesive behind the clear plastic; therefore, all photos are loose and falling out. She pulls some shots close to her face. She has the same poor eyesight that my mother had. Ashlynn squints in the exact manner my mother did by scrunching her eyebrows into her nose. I smile.

"Oh my God, Mom, is this you?" Ashlynn has found a picture of me as a preteen in one of the photo albums. The photo, the epitome of that awkward stage of life, was me at age twelve. I wore braces; my plain brown hair was styled in a mullet, cut short on the sides, spiked on top, and long in the back. My nose—covered in freckles—is surrounded by round, red pimples that were irritated from my obsessive picking. The teeshirt I wore was printed with the word *stretch* across the back—my nickname for being long and lean.

"Yup, that's me. Puberty and all."

"How old were you?"

"Maybe twelve, I'm guessing."

"How old were you when you started your period, Mom?"

"I was twelve."

"How old was I?"

"You were also twelve."

"Do you remember the anatomy book you used to teach me the birds and the bees?" Ashlynn giggles. She likes to hear stories and has asked me when I started my period maybe seven times. Ashlynn likes to listen to repeats of her history and mine. She smiles—always.

"Of course I do. You always responded well to the science behind the way your body works. I found it to be the best way to explain the details."

"Yeah, that's true. You never taught me the slang. So I didn't know what people were talking about at school."

"Oh God. Yeah, I waited to explain that until it came up for you." We giggle.

I glance up at the wall clock above her. We have no place to be, but I'm hyper-focused on mothering, and I must always know if it's near a mealtime. It is only 10:30 a.m. I focus on the beauty of the clock, standing guard on the wall, helping me keep a schedule. It's patient and lovely, and its ticking is a rhythm of consistency. I smile and look away.

We continue flipping through the dozens of photo albums. We both love visiting these collections of our lives, so after we finish going through my mother's, we continue looking through the books of Ashlynn's childhood and the scrapbooks of her life thus far.

Ashlynn has always loved the photos of me while pregnant with her, and all of the stories that accompany them. I adore how this grown child, full of teenage hot-headedness and angst, is still so sweet and in need of love. Not that I have given her a choice in that matter. Love is what I feel; therefore, love is what she shall receive one hundred percent of the time. Whether it's firm or tender—still love.

———

I recall having the conversation about the birds and the bees with my mother. She passed me a pamphlet to read with Casey. Her instructional technique was abrupt and alarming. I was nine, and my brother was seven and a half, our mother was twenty-five. My brother and I sat thigh to thigh on the same couch where Terry almost died.

Mom planted herself in front of us, sitting on the coffee table and picking at the cuticle on her thumb. She raised her thumb to her teeth and ripped off the raised skin. "Shit. I made myself bleed," she said. We suspected terrible news was about to be given. Based on her louder than usual breathing and incessant cuticle picking, she appeared nervous. "It's time you two learned about the birds and the bees."

I had already seen and heard her having sex throughout all of my conscious years and found it to be one of the scariest things I could imagine. And now we were supposed to believe it was a normal part of life? Normal enough to be called the birds and the bees?

She began with, "Has a man ever touched you, Tina? On your privates?" Casey's head whips in my direction.

"No." The idea made me gasp. Was the same thing that happens to her going to happen to me?

"Well, you can't trust any man, so I'm sure it will happen eventually." I looked at my brother. His eyes were wide, and the corners of his mouth turned down. He was as scared as I was.

I could not recall a time when a man had touched my privates, not yet anyway, but I did remember the times our Aunt Berta, my mother's youngest sister, who is only five years older than me, touched my privates. Casey, too, I think. We would "take naps," which the adults used as code for going to have sex. We started saying it too. We would pretend to nap, and our hands would roam on top of our clothes, and our private parts would tingle.

But I was safe with Aunt Berta. She was one of my only friends. I loved and trusted her. It didn't feel wrong or harmful, and I can honestly say it didn't affect me in any negative way that I can identify. She was showing us what she knew. She was showing us what happened to her.

I showed my neighbor, Leanne. We were the same age. We took a nap, and I showed her what my aunt showed me.

"Is this okay?" my neighbor friend asked.

"I think so," I said.

I knew it wasn't acceptable. I understood, somehow, that it was wrong enough that I didn't tell.

"A man raped me when I was eleven," my mother said. "Rape is when someone forces you to have sex with them. I took a walk with this guy. He was a friend of my parents. He said he wanted to be my boyfriend. I liked him. We walked to the baseball field and into the woods to the stream. You know where that stream is?"

"Yes," I whispered.

"He was so cute. He was older. I didn't know what was happening until it was over. If anyone touches you, you should tell me."

"Okay."

"Your father was forced to watch his father molest his sister."

"Aunt Ginny?" I ask. The blood drains from my face.

"Yes. Tarzan's father was so awful. He beat your father and your father's mother and raped Ginny. I think your father ran away when he was twelve. But his mother, Marguerite, was killed. She was hit by a car, then it backed up and ran over her again. Your father knew who did it. He burned their house down."

Wait, I think. *My dad burned his father's house down. Does that mean . . .*

She stands up and leaves us on the couch. She goes to the kitchen and bends over to look in the open refrigerator. "I'm going to write a book someday about my Uncle Joe. He's the one who made me eat ice cream with ants on it. He used to touch me on my privates. And he made me touch him."

She sits at the kitchen table and chews on something. An apple or a piece of lettuce since she's always on a diet, and that's all we ever have in the fridge.

"I have been very sexual from a very young age. My boobs

have been a double D since I was ten. Men always thought I was older. They looked at my boobs and not my face and asked me out all the time. And, Jesus, did I get teased about them in school. My boobs have always been so big."

I glance down at my flat chest. My mother had me called into the nurse's office at school when I was in second grade to have the nurse check them. She told the nurse she wanted to make sure they were typical because although they were tiny, one was more prominent.

The nurse's office announced my mandatory visit over the school intercom. Her office was bright and sunny, with a wall of windows. It was impossible to hide. I joined other kids sitting along the wall when I arrived. She took me into a tiny bathroom and made me take off my shirt. "Lift your arms," she said. I reached for the ceiling and hid my eyes behind my bicep. She pawed at my nonexistent boobs.

When I left the nurse's office, I heard a boy ask, "How's your chest?"

In my memory, the "How Babies Are Made" pamphlet lies on my lap. Tears pool in Casey's eyes and his arms wrap his waist. I raise the white paper for him to see, and we look at the photos. The pictures are black-and-white drawings of a penis inside a vagina, ejaculated sperm, and their journey toward an egg. The next fold of the pamphlet shows the growth of a baby inside a woman and then her spread legs open as she gives birth.

Casey and I sit silently with the pamphlet, the pictures teaching us about how babies are made and born while we listen to our mother describe moments of horror. The ticking of a clock fills the air with its piercing noise. Neither of us knows how to proceed with life now. I fold the paper closed and don't know if I'm supposed to keep it for future reference if I should get raped or molested.

I look to the wall clock making all of the noise in the room. Its minute hand bounces at the peak of each click. A dirtied black plastic circle surrounds a white clock face, now yellowed with cigarette smoke. It seems the loudness of the ticking will knock its cheap plastic-designed self right off the wood-paneled wall.

My brother and I go to our separate tiny trailer bedrooms to digest this new information and wait out our worries.

Why were we brought into this world? I wondered. I know my father was in jail when I was born; he was one week away from turning twenty. When Casey was born, our father, at twenty-one years old, was afraid to look at him because he was worried it would be another girl. Were we simply a burden—baggage to lives more important than our own? Were we a trauma described in one of our mother's dramatic revelations of horrors that earned her bragging rights?

By the time my mother was eighteen, she had been raped; molested by at least one person that I knew of; had two children; been married and divorced; and, in her opinion, was the focus of every man's sexual desire. The father of her children, my father, was having sex with her sister, and she had witnessed more drunken brawls between her parents and their friends than I could keep straight.

She had witnessed her father threaten her mother's life with a shotgun to her head for being unfaithful—another of many examples of rage induced by his jealousy. Since then, Mom's younger brother, Bobby, has had a stutter. In more recent years I learned that my grandmother might have also slept with my father—an estranged girlfriend of my father's sent a Facebook message to Ashlynn describing the details of his relationship with my grandmother. An accusation my father was aware of that he neither addressed nor denied.

Maybe Aunt Berta is my half sister? She's the only sibling of my mother's that has green eyes like me. As far as I know, a blue eyed parent matched with a brown eyed parent cannot have a green eyed child. Berta is five years older than me. My father would have been a teenager and my grandmother had to be in her late twenties or early thirties. If in fact, Berta is my half sister, since Aunt Berta's mother is my grandmother, is she more than just a half sister? Do I really want to know?

———

I shake my head and push away these memories. I hold one of my current life's photo albums in my hands and return my eyes to the beautiful antique clock on our living room wall. In contrast to the one in the trailer from my youth, this clock's ticking is pleasurable—quiet and composed. I picked it up at Goodwill a few months back, and I adore its crackled white finish and the large base that it sits on. The clock's composure settles my racing heart.

I cannot imagine telling my daughter such traumatic stories, let alone at such a young age. Her coming into this world was a product of love, and I will go to my grave showing her that there are beautiful kinds of love in this world. Types of love that she is worthy of, and so am I.

Chapter Seven

Comfort

After perusing the dozens of photo albums between my mother's and mine, Ashlynn and I look through the final album together. As we close the last page, Ashlynn asks, "Where are Grammy's drawings?"

"In the attic," I say.

We decide to visit the pastel and charcoal drawings my mother had compiled throughout her life. She'd been an artist since her childhood, signing all her works with *Diane Davis* until her forties—in her later years, she drew a collection of portraits signed with a simple *Di*.

We climb the stairs to the attic and flick on the lights. I pull the leather art bag from a box of my mother's things and pass it to Ashlynn. She finds a clear spot on the floor amidst dozens of boxes of holiday decorations, settling herself between the Halloween and Easter containers.

I retrieve the collection of larger drawings that are secured between two pieces of cardboard and join her on the floor.

First, we find the face of Sylvester Stallone, then Brook Shields, Prince, and Michael Jackson, all in pastels. Next, we uncover a poster-sized pastel of my mother's youngest sister,

Berta. She was the youngest of five siblings, a lost soul, and as desperate for love as all of them. I often wonder who molested her. Who showed her what she showed my brother and me? The roaming hands over our clothes to the privates of her niece and nephew.

Then we find another poster-sized portrait. An oil painting this time—Mom's father. My grandfather. Ashlynn's great-grampy. A man I have never felt a single ounce of love for; however, a man doted on by all of his children. A cold, mean man who never hugged, kissed, or told any of his children or grandchildren that he loved them. My grandfather was mad all of the time. What I remember most about him was his yelling at my brother and my grandmother. My grandmother would roll her eyes and respond, "Jesus, Bobby."

After my beloved grandmother died when I was twenty-five, I felt like I lost the only grandparent I ever had. My maternal grandmother is the only grandparent that showed me love. Gentle, quiet love. A hug, a lap to sit on, and a birthday card every year. My grandfather was desperate to move on and find a new partner as soon as she died. It felt disgusting, and it proved to me how weak he was.

He commented on every woman and child's weight in the family. "What you got under there, a spare tire?" He would say to anyone who wasn't stick thin. He complimented me on my thinness, and I hated it. He compared me to my aunt and mother right in front of us. "Jesus, Diane, you've put on a few, haven't you?"

My grandfather's vocabulary was evidence of an under

educated man. He was a self centered bigot who used words like: dyke and nigger, to express negative judgment.

My paternal grandparents both died a week into my life. They were in their forties. My mother told me they only held me once.

Why would she paint her father's portrait? Why not her mother's? My beautiful grandmother, Gloria—breathtaking light blue eyes and long dirty blonde hair. She let me brush her hair whenever I wanted, and she loved animals, rescuing all that needed her—even wild animals. She adopted a baby crow and named him Igor. Orphaned baby squirrels, chipmunks, mice, and a raccoon named Ricky—all saved by her.

I find the oil painting my brother did of our grandfather's lobster boat. It's the only oil painting he has ever done and it's such a fantastic likeness. Casey is a painting genius. He's always been good at many things. His IQ was determined to be genius level, and he is witty and sweet—always has been. Casey needed love and guidance probably more than I did, and it was lacking. After he began showing noticeable signs of not doing well emotionally, our mother agreed to cook dinner once a week. She chose Sunday. It didn't last.

This lobster boat painting depicts a small white vessel rolling over large waves. Casey captured the coldness in the ocean and the heartbeat of the waves against the wooden boat. *Comfort* was the boat's name. While Ashlynn continues to flip through my mother's drawings, I study my brother's painting. The time my grandfather and uncle were lost at sea begins to play in my mind.

———

I can see the ocean. I can smell its salty pungency. My grandfather's lobster boat dips right and left while anchored at a lone mooring in Frenchmen's Bay. Gentle ocean ripples caress its wooden mass. I kick off my flip-flops and wade into the shallow water that's so cold my feet instantly go numb. No surprise. I caress the salty water with my fingertips as I wade toward *Comfort*, minding the sharp, barnacled rocks by following an erratic path of soft muck.

My mother bathes in the sunshine at the bay's edge, and her confidence in my eight-year-old self invigorates my own. Never a worry or a "Be careful," breathed from her lips, except for when she's scolding me for getting hurt, always saying, "You should've been more careful." She has a negligent expectation of tenacity and perseverance in her children.

I wonder why my grandfather has chosen to name his lobster boat *Comfort*. Isn't that a woman's name? Or a feeling? Maybe he feels protected from the vast ocean, certain he is out of danger inside a female sea vessel. But that would mean he's vulnerable—something he would never admit.

The icy water of low tide reddens the skin of my thighs as I reach the stern. I trace the layers of painted letters with the wetness on my fingertips; a stream of clear water cascades down my forearm and awakens goosebumps. The faded black paint darkens at my hydrating touch. I copy the letters with my saltwater finger paint—*Comfort*.

My grandfather and his eldest son, Forrest, who works as

his first mate, remove buckets of aged bait from the truck parked behind my mother's car. They carry the full buckets to the water and load them into a small dingy, its bow sinking into the soft earth at the shore. The smell of rotten fish wafts through the air without warning. I pinch my nose with slippery fingers and make my way back to my napping mother. I find a small space on the corner of her white sheet and sit down, making sure not to disturb or crowd her. Casey crouches over the rocks, playing with the two small trucks.

My grandfather waves at me. A rare gesture of awareness of my presence. I smile. Surprise presses my eyebrows together, and I wave back. He shakes his head and laughs at me. Then I realize he was trying to get my unresponsive mother's attention. I drop my eyes to my feet.

The two men pull their folded rubber boots up to the tops of their thighs, and they, too, wade in. They push the small dingy through the calm sea. The tide is so low they walk out to *Comfort*, just like I did. Forrest climbs aboard, and my grandfather passes him the buckets of foul bait. Now loaded and ready for an afternoon of lobster fishing, they release *Comfort's* ropes and tie the dingy in her place at the mooring.

Comfort's engine spits and sputters, and she drifts close to shore, endangering the motor with impact on rocks. After multiple attempts, she responds, and her deep and throaty growls spit clouds of dark gray smoke into the air. My Uncle Forrest whips her around starboard and sends teasing round waves at us. He salutes a silent goodbye with a flat hand pressed to his forehead. My mother is sound asleep and un-aware. I return his smile.

I rub my palm against the sticky pitch on my elbow—evidence of yesterday's tree climb. My mother's breathing is heavy, and her relaxed lips part enough to show the edges of her front teeth. I pull at the pitch on my elbow and succeed at removing a small amount, which glues itself to my fingers instead. I pull it up to my nose and inhale the sweet scent of pine.

I lie back onto the rocks warmed by the sun, and my eyes scan the landscape. Long brown tree trunks surround Frenchmen's Bay; they are tall and muscular and remind me of a guardsman protecting this tranquil harbor. Their limbs, covered in sharp pine needles, sway with elegance as a cool breeze puffs off the ocean. I can imagine the tickle of the foliage against my skin and the whisper of the wind through their branches beckoning me, "Come play with us."

I inhale the pine smell once again; it reminds me of a patient, towering, and trusted friend whose exquisite perseverance has earned her a blanket of stunning green needles that remains all winter. An undying beauty and strength are shared and imprinted on the people of Maine.

As it often happens without warning, cool fog rolls onto shore from the ocean and masks the sun. It moves fast upon us, and I imagine the fog is Mother Nature's ghost crowding out the sun. Our restfulness is shocked into arousal, and my mother jumps up and dashes for her car. I pick up all of her belongings and follow with Casey in tow.

We return home to my grandparents' at First South Street wrapped in a white sheet shared across the front seats. The fog followed us here, and the air is thickened by the blur of clouds that have settled onto the earth. I realize my flip-flops were left behind at the bay and will, without a doubt, be lost at sea when the tide comes in.

The squeaking screen door welcomes us into our family's unnamed home, a place more befitting of the title *Comfort* than my grandfather's boat. The smell of overheated coffee and wood fire wraps around me like a favorite blanket. I climb under the couch's afghan and stare up at the colorful stained-glass window high above the wooden stairs that lead to the second floor. Within moments, I fall asleep.

I wake later in the evening to find Casey snuggled close beside me, and voices wincing with distress from the dining room. I blink open my dry eyes and slink out from under the afghan, careful not to wake my brother. I make my way to the dining room and crawl into my grandmother's lap.

She's sitting in her regular place at the top of the table. She spoons two heaping scoops of sugar into a clay cup filled with black coffee and pours in so much cream that the dark brown liquid turns the color of caramel candy. She stirs the contents into a miniature whirlpool within her cup, then clinks the spoon on the side of the mug. I lean in and wrap my lips over the edge of the cup and suck in the first sweet sip. When I finish, my grandmother lifts the cup to her mouth, and she takes a long drink.

The conversation around me reveals the cause of today's

ruin. Another familiar and disappointing loss of quietness caused by the volatile and unhealthy relationships around me; however, my good sense always reminds me that their disarray is caused by the choices my family makes, and I remain silent and ignored—my safe place.

My grandfather and Uncle Forrest have not returned from their afternoon of lobster fishing. It is now so late in the day that the sky is black, and the fog remains thick and blinding. My grandmother and their other four children surround the oval dining room table. The only conclusion circling the group is the possibility of drowning, and all of a sudden, the grumpy old man they each fear and sometimes hate becomes someone they love and miss. As usual, I'm confused by this family's hypocritical and convoluted points of view.

I am not worried. My grandfather and my uncle are cradled in the ocean by a boat named *Comfort*, and in her arms, they will safely be. I am sure of it. I have not one ounce of doubt. I can't imagine that a man so hardened and adept at survival would do anything but survive.

I listen to the doubts served on the long table that night, and I imagine I am old and wise enough to tell them the truth. The truth of who we are, who he is, and how there is no way he won't find his way home from being lost at sea in the fog.

After all, this one night, adrift with a camouflaged navigation system, would never be the end of him. I'm sure this cannot be the first time he's been on the ocean with zero visibility off all directions of the stern, port, and starboard sides.

A man such as my grandfather would know the specific focus of the waves toward shore. He would understand the call of the seagulls, and he would learn to hold firm until the giant pine trees return to view, welcoming him back to port. He is a man much too weathered and worn to let this be the end of him.

His American Indian tribal ancestors from our small town of Bar Harbor embody the women and men who prove each day that oppression only exists if allowed, and the understanding that hard work is a daily necessity that anyone is capable of. His foster home and family, whose cruelty forced him to harness his animalistic survival instincts, and my grandmother, Gloria, who wrapped him in her able arms and gave him five children, are all reasons he will find his way home.

Twenty-four hours of fog, no word from my grandfather, and no sightings of them by the Coast Guard turn to forty-eight hours. He is still lost. Could I have been wrong? Is it possible he will never return?

I walk the length of First South Street to its end and peer toward the town bustling with tourists. Each summer, our narrow streets and favorite restaurants become cluttered with unfamiliar faces, and we squeeze our way through town trying to go about our lives.

Today I stay near home and feel grateful for the blue-painted screened-in porch where I can sit and wait. I lay on the prehistoric orange couch stained with spilled lemonade and ice cream and press my feet against the screen wall. The restaurant next door has grown so far into our space that I can touch it with my toes if I push hard enough on the screen.

———

Ashlynn finds a glossy page torn out of a magazine—a shirtless, full upper body image of Elvis. "Grammy loved Elvis, didn't she?" Ashlynn holds up the shiny paper.

"Oh my God, yes. Elvis was pretty handsome, and everyone loved him. I remember when he died. I was six years old and riding my bike on First South Street, wondering why everyone was so upset?"

"He was an icon."

"Yes, I figured that out as I got older."

It was how I felt when my grandfather had gone missing. I didn't understand why everyone was so upset. Regardless, it had become another reason for everyone to ignore me. I sink back into my reflection on the time he was lost at sea.

———

I hear my mother's worried voice and head back inside. I find her on the opposite porch behind the house, just steps away from my grandmother's clam-shucking shed. She's holding a cigarette in one hand and white tissue in the other. I caress her long brown hair and pull it back from her face. She's debating the chances of losing her father with Sandra, her older sister, and their brown eyes fill with tears that drain down their cheeks—the dimple in the center of my mother's chin quivers. I continue to pat and pull back her hair in an attempt to caress her worries away with my touch.

If her cries escalate beyond the chin quiver, I cannot keep up my attempts of consolation. Lucky for me, tears and the chin quiver are as far as it gets. Not that I have ever been able to console her. I accept her unawareness of my presence as normalcy.

I still believe their worry is in vain.

A sudden ring of the house phone brings everyone to their feet. My grandmother presses the receiver to her ear. I fix my eyes on the swaying of the dirty yellow cord. I breathe in and out, making sure not to rush my breaths, and wrap my arms around my waist. My mother hangs onto her older sister's shoulders, while the other two siblings, Bobby Junior and Berta, hug each other with their faces pressed toward their mother. Berta's green eyes are wide with fear. Casey is sitting alone on the floor. He leans his back against the cabinet door and hugs his knees—a matchbox car in each hand.

My grandmother holds her hand over her heart; her eyes and mouth are wide, she listens. She turns from us and we rush to face her, hoping for good news. Her cheeks redden, and her eyes close. Tears drip onto her white blouse and fore-arm.

It appears they were right. I cannot believe it. There's no way he could be gone, lost forever. I will fiercely disagree with whoever says different. My grandfather could not ever die at sea.

A smile spreads across my grandmother's face, and she moves her hand from her heart to her mouth. Through her fingers, I hear her say, "The Coast Guard found them."

"He should've been more careful," says my mother with a huff.

———

Ashlynn holds up a cartoonish sketch my mother did of Betty Boop. "This would be a cool tattoo," she says.

"Oh geez," I respond.

———

Perhaps one day I'll lose the memory of how my grandfather and uncle got lost at sea, but I will never forget the day we learned the news of their survival. The story I told myself was about the tall pine trees surrounding Otter Creek calling to them as they did to me just two days earlier with their wind whispers and pine bouquet. As the sun burned away the fog, the first thing the men in the boat would have seen is their mighty girth and familiar triangular peaks announcing land.

I remember imagining how comforting it must have been for my Uncle Forrest and my grandfather to behold the determined welcoming of such an ally. The pines, too, have survived—like the jagged coast surmounting a victorious battle against the manic sea.

I know my grandfather wasn't considering the fact that he may never see me again. I know he didn't care if I was worried or upset. I'm sure I didn't even enter his mind. The next time I see him, it will be like he was never gone, and I won't exist.

———

I snap back to present day in the attic as Ashlynn asks, "Is that Casey's painting, Mom?"

"Yes, honey, it is. Isn't it good?"

"It's so good. That's Great-Grampy's lobster boat, right?"

"Yes, it is. Casey is so talented."

"Well, he did become a painter. Of houses, anyway."

"True. Casey is sharing his talent in other ways." I smile and wink at Ashlynn.

Chapter Eight

Stained-Glass Window

Billy, Ashlynn, and I pull into a small parking lot—tiny compared to the giant brick building it services. Parking in Portland is scarce, so this petit square of dirt will have to do. Billy chooses a tight spot that overhangs the sidewalk, leaving just enough room for me to open the door and get out without bumping into the minivan parked next to us. We scan the aged, antique-filled, five-story stone masterpiece. Portland has many impressive buildings.

This one houses a business that sells salvaged pieces of antique homes. Substantial parts of historic houses: mantels, doors, windows, and light fixtures. And littles, which are smaller, lower-priced items, like trinkets, knickknacks, doorknobs, locks, and hardware.

We enter the first floor. The wood beneath our feet creaks at our arrival. No one greets us. I smile. We hear faint voices far away in the vast building. A wood-burning cook stove covered in rust and flaking white paint sits to my right. I attempt to lift it to see how heavy it is. It doesn't move. Billy laughs. "You try," I say. He lifts the corner from the floor with ease. "Jesus," I say.

I take the lead, and Billy and Ashlynn follow at my heels. Ashlynn soon heads off on her own to look at old books. She always makes sure to keep an eye out for Hardy Boys and Nancy Drew novels. Billy shops at my pace, and he offers an abundance of knowledge for objects I've never seen before—always the trivia winner. Once we reach the old doors for sale, he takes off, now shopping on his own.

I look up. No one ever does, but I always do. Giant light fixtures with aged brass and glass dangle in silence above us. Dust dulls their finish, and I categorize them as being worthy of a castle. I have learned they are way out of my price range at thousands of dollars each. Stained-glass windows hang with an artful touch between each of the dozens of light fixtures.

I trip on the uneven floorboards and look down just long enough to see where I'm walking. There are hundreds of beautiful windows. I have only ever lived with the stained-glass window at my grandparents' house on First South Street. I would fall asleep on the couch, staring at it high above the staircase. Like I did the day my grandfather got lost in the fog at sea. Ours had square panes of dark blue, red, brown, and yellow glass surrounding one pane of clear textured glass in the center. The surrounding wood was dark, and a matching window at the bottom of the stairs was out of view from the couch.

I remember the vivid colors would blur as sleepiness took over. I would fall asleep and wake to its beauty. The stained-glass window was a comforting sight even when the sounds around me were not so pleasant. When cigarette smoke and alcohol vapors clouded the living room, wafting in from the whiskey table in the kitchen where arguments consumed the grown-ups in the house while the children were ignored—until they weren't, when an adult had ill intentions or roaming hands.

"Lay behind the couch so the men won't bother you," my mother would say during drunken parties at the house. I made sure I could still see the colorful window from my hiding spot.

———

The prices for these salvaged windows are exorbitant. I've given up hope on finding one that will fit into my price range. I enjoy the sight of them even so. I study each one, and if I squint hard enough, I can read the price tag. My neck begins to ache from its arched position, with my chin pointing away from my chest.

I near the staircase to the second floor, so I climb up. On my way up the stairs, I find smaller stained-glass pieces and some small windows hanging on the wall. I see a perfect square window measuring eighteen by eighteen in a wooden frame. The white paint flakes off here and there revealing layers of colors underneath; the six panes of colored glass are each a quilt square design containing colored triangles. Within every other pane, the color pattern alternates from red-and-yellow to green-and-yellow. A white sticker reads two hundred and seventy-five dollars.

I remove it from the wall and put it under my armpit. I smile. I feel as if I have just won a victory in a battle against my past. I have a new stained-glass window that I can adore—one whose beauty will not be overshadowed by a fighting family, the turmoil of intoxication, or the indecency of their acquaintances. With this, I can now come to terms with more moments from my youth. My bicep burns under the window's weight, and I compare it to carrying my baby. It doesn't matter how much it hurts. I'm never putting you down.

I continue walking through the store with my eyes now pointed down toward the items on the floor, tables, and benches. I no longer need to look up. I have my gold medal.

I think about my grandfather. Hate burns in my subconscious. My mother was so young when we were born that we lived with her parents most of the time. Once in a while, my mother would try to make it on her own. But we would always go back—between apartments, towns, and relationships. She spent a lot of time with her father. She took us blueberry picking, clamming, fishing, to the beach; wherever he was, we would follow.

The terror of the day I got into a boat with him after his time lost at sea regurgitates itself into my mind. This particular day wasn't one filled with joy—that never was the case. This boat ride happened on one of the many days when my fear was met with derision by those around me. It was another day when those who should have been protecting me didn't even care that I was there. Again, it was as if I were a piece of glass, and this was another day that shattered me.

The pain that radiated from my core that day comes back, accompanied by the bitter cold only an ocean can provide, and the fear within a child that can only be caused by the lack of empathy from those I should've been able to trust the most.

————

The ocean salt settles in my nose, and I play at the shore. My mother searches for sea glass while my grandfather works in the velvety mud, digging for clams. I avoid the clam flats as the heavy earth sucks at my feet, and I would inevitably lose a shoe. I dance over the rocks, using rugged barnacles to secure my footing.

I find the perfect spot on the edge of the water where I can reach the seaweed to search for crabs. I lift the lengthy stalks and pop the seawater out of the round fluid-filled pockets in the seaweed. An angry crab raises his open claw at me as he hurries away, crawling sideways.

The wind whips, and I keep pulling my hair out of my mouth. It tastes salty. I decide to face the wind so it blows my hair back instead of into my face. I shiver under my teeshirt and shorts, but if I crouch down low, the wind misses me, and my body warms.

I hear the loud sound of metal scraping metal as my grandfather pulls the dingy from the back of his truck bed. My mother approaches me. As soon as she's close enough for me to hear her call, she says, "C'mon, Tina, we're heading across the bay."

I stand up, dry my hands on my shorts, and slip my wet feet into my sneakers. My sockless toes rub against grains of sand inside my shoes as I follow my mother to the boat. I wrap a bright orange life vest around my shoulders. It's already wet and the dampness adds to my chill. I shiver. I secure the plastic clip around my waist and hold my mother's hand, then we wade into the water together. Forceful waves push against me. I grab onto her hand with both of mine. The wind creates ripples within ripples on the water, like goosebumps on the ocean. At the peak of each wave, a salty rain sprays at my face.

I'm afraid to get into the boat and afraid to cross the bay. The ocean looks angry and could still be out to get my grandfather. My mother instructs me to get into the boat first. I grab onto the cold metal seat with a hand on either side of my knees. I look at my grandfather with wide eyes, realizing I have no say in this. My mother climbs in next and sits beside me. I can see the patch of land we're boating to on the other side of the large waves erupting from the sea. "It's not too far," I say to myself with an unconvincing quiver in my voice.

My grandfather wades into the water and pushes us off the shore. He steps inside the boat, causing it to tip to one side. I inhale so quickly it creates a whistle, and I crouch into my hands, gripping my body to the seat. He puffs a disgusted breath at me while he sits in the middle of the boat with an oar in each hand. Once we're far enough from shore, he sets the oars inside the vessel and goes to the small motor behind him. The boat dips so far to the right and left that I can see under the next wave rising toward us.

I inhale a quick breath and widen my arms and press my elbows out away from my body as I squeeze the seat with my hands. My grandfather spits laughter at me. The motor starts, and we begin to move toward the whitecaps and into the unsettled bay. I feel the tingling of panic travel through my limbs. I cry, my face turns red, and my eyes widen with every incline and decline the tiny boat makes as it crossed each mountainous wave.

My grandfather laughs at me with his mouth wide open.

"I don't want to go," I cry out, but the overpowering noise of the motor silences my voice. It roars like a monster. I can't even look at my mother. If I take my eyes off the bottom of the boat, I'm sure I'll lose my grip and be tossed out. I hear another eruption of laughter from my grandfather.

Another wave. "Ahhh," I scream, continuing my panicked cry. "I don't want to go." My mother says nothing. My eyes raise from the bottom of the silver boat to my grandfather's face. His toothless smile reveals one molar on the right side of his top arch. His mouth widens, and he laughs at me again.

I hate him.

I know the meanness in him is what saved him from being lost at sea, but I'm not so sure about me. I'm petite and insignificant. I will get tossed around helpless to the power of the ocean, and if I'm ever found, I'll be waterlogged, smashed by pounding waves, and my skin blued by the freezing saltwater.

But most likely I will be lost forever at sea, just like the flip-flops I left behind the day the fog rolled in, and my mother raced ahead to her car.

My body is rigid, I feel helpless and drowned, and I'm shaking with fear. Cold consumes my fingers that have gone white as they remain clenched around the edge of the metal boat, and I ache all over. I want to be home. Warm. I want to be away from this moment, but I have nowhere to escape. I have no one to help me. Hold me. Comfort me. I become invisible to myself—a shell. My heart feels so big and painful that my chest could break open.

My mother spits out a huff. This singular noise says so many things. At this moment, her pronounced exhale explains her disgust in my lack of bravery. She's bothered by my neediness and has no tolerance for me being scared of a damn boat ride. I can imagine her saying, "Jesus Christ, Tina. It's a five-minute boat ride."

It might have only lasted five minutes, but it felt as though that boat ride would never end and I truly thought the ocean would pluck me from the small vessel and deliver me to my death in the ice-cold water. We finally make it through the angry stretch of water and reach the other side of the bay. My feet meet the stable ground with adoration, and I kneel down to touch the soft mud with my hands. I put my chin to my knees and take deep breaths.

There's a pain in my chest I cannot describe—anger mixed with fear. It lingers like an injury. Like the radiating pain I felt when I broke my ankle. Excruciating pain I could barely breathe through and that I thought would be the end of me. But I had to go on. I had no choice but to continue to live through this moment. I had no escape.

Time stood still.

My mother and grandfather walk away from me, leaving me at the ocean's edge—as if nothing had happened. So of course, like any child, I feel shame. I assume it's me that's the problem. I must be wrong and weak for being scared. If I were braver, this wouldn't hurt so bad. It's all my fault.

And yet, I don't want to get back in that boat. Mom and Grampa can go back without me. I will stay here and wait until the wind quiets and the ocean smooths. I fear its mood will not matter, and Mommy will force me to make the trek back through.

I recall nothing from the rest of the day.

I tell myself that someone or something helped me. I tell myself that the wind died, the sun prevailed, and the ocean settled into its beautiful mirror of the sky for our return trip. The calm waters only needed the muscle of the oars to return us to our truck and then on to home. I imagine that my mother hugged me until the pain in my chest subsided and that she did something to protect me from this cold man—my grandfather. I hope for my sake that is what happened in the end. If it wasn't, I haven't allowed myself to remember otherwise.

After that day, bouncy houses gave me the same panicked feeling of being on the sea with my grandfather. An innocent, fun childhood experience—bouncy houses. I couldn't go in.

If I did, I clung to the rubber floor with both hands and knees and couldn't stand up, let alone jump. The instability drove me to such panic once that I yelled at a little girl and her father, telling them, "STOP JUMPING. I can't stand up. I want to get out." They ignored me and kept jumping. I suspect my fear of Ferris wheels comes from the same place.

———

"Oh, that's cool," says Billy, pointing to the window under my arm.

"Did you find any old doors you can use for projects?" I ask.

"Yeah, but they're costly. The prices are high here."

"They are, but I lucked out today. I'm going to get this window."

Ashlynn approaches with an antique washbowl and pitcher set. "Can I get this? It's seventy-nine dollars."

"That's beautiful. And it's decorated with peonies, your favorite," I say.

"Yes, you can get it. I'm buying," says Billy. I kiss him. Billy is generous in every way humanly possible. He's very giving with his love, his time, gifts, and laughter. And although I know these things, I often ask myself if perhaps Billy gives these gifts out of guilt. Maybe he wants to make up for infidelity, lying, or regret.

I shake away this insecurity and take his hand in mine. "Thank you, Billy. That's so sweet of you," I say.

Chapter Nine

Dancing Queen

It's a rainy Sunday. Ashlynn, Billy, and I eat our lunch in the living room—tuna melts on pretzel buns with raw carrots and cucumbers instead of chips. *Mamma Mia*, the movie, is playing on our TV. Ashlynn gave me the DVD, along with a bonus DVD of *Xanadu*, starring Olivia Newton-John, for Mother's Day a few years back—two of my favorite movies.

Ashlynn is in the oversized chair with the bulldog, of course, and her outstretched legs are propped up on the ottoman that we purchased for this exact purpose—lounging. The chubby, gray bulldog drools over her knees and watches her eat the sandwich. The other, better-behaved dog is asleep on the floor.

Meryl Streep discovers that the three potential fathers of her daughter are hiding in her loft. The song "Mamma Mia" breaks out. Ashlynn and I set our plates aside and leap from our spots to dance. The bulldog is annoyed. We sway our hips and arms and sing the words at a volume above the television. Billy exits the room, leaving us to our fun.

The dog steps off the lounge chair and onto the coffee table—his favorite place to be when insisting we pay attention to him. He barks and growls at us as we gambol around the room.

We laugh and continue our dance.

Ashlynn and I clasp hands and twirl each other in circles. Once the song is over, we flop back into our respective reclining positions to watch the rest of the movie. We're both a little out of breath but still take bites of our food and chew with open mouths. The dog steps off the coffee table and returns to snuggling with Ashlynn and watching her eat.

I am happy.

This movie introduces an uncanny innocence to the concept of multiple male partners and not knowing who the father of your child is. And the fact that the father could be any one of the three men remained a secret to prevent them from being hurt. Keeping secrets for the sake of not hurting people is so different from how I grew up. Romantic even. That was never the case for my mother.

Not that I suggest dishonesty of any kind—dishonesty scares me. I consider it more like a means of protecting your children. As I can attest, a child seeing and hearing violence is awful—the trauma scars. And yet, the scars are open wounds that remain on the verge of infection throughout life.

Does infidelity not have to be scary? The other men in this movie aren't fighting. There's a distinct lack of blood, death threats, or the police. Maybe it can be lighthearted, or perhaps I'm just a fool for believing in a movie. Well, at least Ashlynn doesn't seem upset about it.

The movie continues. As always, my mind drifts back to

my childhood. I remember taking the bulldog's position and dancing on the coffee table. I would dress in one of my mother's lacy camisoles and don a Halloween mask, but only when my father or his company would arrive.

I have so few memories of him being present in my childhood and teenage life—only a handful of memories, but enormous and impactful in their presence.

―――――

My coffee table entertaining began after witnessing my father and some of his friends watch a 1970s movie of a woman dancing. She must have been sexy, because she had tiny clothes on and my father whistled at her. I can still see the light skin of her body in the spotlight, and the dark crowd around her. If I could see it again today, I would know it right away. The film excited my father. He gave it his undivided attention; he made comments, whistled, and seemed happy as he watched it. I tried for the same effect. It worked.

I was three, maybe four years old the first time I put on my mother's sexy nightie and a mask to change my identity, hoping to gain my parents' attention. My father paid attention to me. He whistled and laughed. He encouraged me to continue and told everyone about it. I was the center of his attention. This younger version of myself—before the days of playing waitress—loved it. These were days in New Jersey, near the time of my mother's heartbreak.

I continued to try to be part of their world. I moved my spotlight dancing from the coffee table to a round leather footstool. It was a deep burgundy color and didn't have the clutter of ashtrays and beer cans. That became my new stage.

As I continued to emulate the moments in my parents' world that retained most of their focus, I started dipping into the ashtrays, taking matches and chewing off the sulfur wicks. Is it possible I was just hungry? For the most part, I believe it was me trying to be part of their life. I know I was hungry for their love. To try and feed that hunger, I noticed what their favorite things were and immersed myself within them. Cigarettes, alcohol, and each other were a few of their favorite things, but not me.

––––––

"Ashlynn, can I get you something for dessert, honey?"

"No, Mom, I'm perfect."

"I already know that, sweet girl."

The song "Dancing Queen" spirits us out of our reclining positions and back onto the floor to dance again. The dog perches himself on the coffee table and moans at us—his claws, cushioned by the thick pads of his round feet, don't make a scratch. Although the aged wooden top of the coffee table was already scratched into a vintage beauty and would hide any marks, I'm sure he would add if he could. The white crackled paint on the pine legs makes it appear to be metal and not wood. Our lack of cigarette smoking and regular alcohol consumption leaves our coffee table cluttered with nothing but remote controls.

As "Dancing Queen" ends, Ashlynn and I return to our

spots. We share a love of musicals. Her ballet career introduced me to classical music and an appreciation for the performing arts. Another favorite of ours, *Phantom of the Opera*, has the same effect on us, as well as the dog.

———

Dancing with my mother was not quite the same. A more appropriate title for that would be *Demons at the Disco*. "Let's go dancing, Tina" meant going to the club, drinking far too much, and my mother leaving with a different man each time. I was underage. It didn't matter. The bouncers all knew her and let me in without question. Soon I learned some of the men she took home were actually boys—my friends from high school.

It would begin with the proud look in their eyes when she brought them over to me; shame would rise in the pit of my stomach as I saw their hands resting on the top of her buttocks, followed by rage that I could feel boiling beneath my face. And, beyond that, I felt something unexpected: fear.

My mother having sex with my acquaintances from high school filled me with fear. The kind of fear that makes you want to faint or run. The fear you feel when you realize you have zero people on your side—not a single person in this world who would fight for you, who would hold your truths as universal and untouchable. I had no one willing to do that for me. The only people that are supposed to are at least your parents. But not mine.

During this time, I began having nightmares of my mother

having sex with my boyfriend. It felt so authentic and possible, as if the injury had occurred, and now I was faced with the impossible task of moving on.

For years I wished she would grow up. I was hopeful at every one of her birthdays that she was maturing as she got older. I waited for a mother who would protect me and be wise enough to guide me. I wished she would get old so she would stop drinking and sleeping around.

———

The sound of splashing water returns my focus to *Mamma Mia*. A young Merrill Streep dives into the ocean from the boat of one of the possible fathers of her daughter. The movie, set in Greece, focuses on the beauty of the Aegean Sea; however, to me, the ocean is the ocean. And for some odd reason, I think of John Grant. I suspect it was the ocean and the thoughts of dancing at a bar with my mother that brought him back. This night, the last time I recall John Grant hijacking my sense of safety and my mother's good sense, was on a night the smell of the ocean was potent in the air that was thickened with fog.

———

One summer night in Bar Harbor, between my junior and senior year in college, we—myself, Casey, our mother, Uncle Forrest, and Aunt Laurie—were in a bar together.

"John Grant's here," my mother spit out. She stood so close to me I could smell the alcohol on her breath.

"Where?" I asked.

"Forget it, Tina, let's just go."

"No, Mom. Where is he? I need to see him." She pointed him out.

I froze, shocked. "What?" I see a gray-haired, wobbling drunk man. Gravity pulled the skin of his face toward the floor. His squinted eyes were so small he appeared half-asleep on his feet. He was shorter than me and unaware of our presence.

I walked up to face him. He had no idea who I was. A half-smile crinkles the sagging skin around his right eye, closing it. My chest heaved with my attempts to not burst out crying. I wanted to push him. I wanted to start a bar fight. The hair on my head stood up, and my ears twitched. I raised one of my eyebrows and scowled at him.

I was standing in front of the man who shot my father. I was inches from the real-life boogeyman of my nightmares. He was still drinking in the bars in Bar Harbor, and by the looks of him, he had never stopped. He smelt like stale beer and the sweetness of alcoholic ketoacidosis—that dirty and sickly smell caused by the overconsumption of alcohol and his body's desperate attempt to metabolize it all. I imagined his brain floating in a sea of beer and his drowning pores spitting more out.

I did nothing. But not out of fear. I did nothing because it would not have made a difference. John Grant had no idea who I was, and he was not worth it. Instead, I became angry at my mother. She had betrayed me so many times in different ways throughout my life. This drunken man was evidence of another betrayal—my sense of safety.

Again.

John Grant was an old drunk man. He was not a man I should have spent my whole life being afraid of. I wanted to cry. I wanted to flee my mother and her drinking.

And I did.

I tried to distance myself from it and her. But Mom wouldn't let me. Instead, she brought more injury to me.

———

Mamma Mia's three potential fathers came together for one girl. And though they were each absent for most of their daughter's life, she welcomed them in with love, as if they had always been there. My father's been absent for most of my life, but I welcome him in whenever he's willing to be involved. My mother hated it, and yet, she never stopped loving him.

I suspect John Grant lingered in her subconscious because he brought my father and her together. This connection between them and John Grant was unhealthy but potent.

———

My mind spins off on its own again, traveling away from *Mamma Mia* and heading to times when my mother used other men to gain my father's attention—not just John Grant. I was a newlywed in this particular memory, like the girl in *Mamma Mia* would soon be.

I married Ashlynn's biological father, Lance, in 1996.

In 1998, my father began building us a house tucked away from the world in a small town called Pownal—one of Maine's many rural hideaways.

On one particular weekend, my father, Lance, and I were working on the structure that we would someday call home. It was a quiet day at our build site, and my dad's usual crew of workers wasn't there. We huddled around a wooden picnic table, discussing our project while my father smoked cigarettes, and I drank a Diet Coke.

I was twenty-six; my mother was two months from her forty-first birthday.

My mother arrived with her younger sister, Berta, and a male friend—a boy. I assumed he was with Berta. But my mother soon made it clear he was with her.

I was proud of our work, and I began explaining where we were in the process of building. My mother didn't even pretend to listen; instead, she swooned into the eyes of the boy. Her shirt exposed her midsection. The top button on her jeans was undone, and the edges of her pants folded over. She traced the pale skin just above her jeans with her fingertips, pressing them just under the edge of her waistband and sweeping them along the edge of her pants. The boy's eyes followed her hand. He looked up at her face.

Their eye contact was intense, and it made my stomach turn. My face boiled with anger. The success of our project was irrelevant to her. She had come to visit for an entirely different reason.

I stopped talking and examined her behavior. It all became clear. She'd brought this very young man here to flaunt him in front of my father, making it apparent that she was having sex with him.

"What did you say your name was?" I asked the boy.

"Jerry," he said.

"What year did you graduate from high school?" I ask.

"In 1996," he said.

"So you're younger than me? What are you doing with her, then?" I ask. His brown skin reddened.

"Tina!" My mother said. "How dare you?"

"I just don't understand what he's doing with you. He's younger than me, Mom. By seven years."

"I don't have to take this shit," my mother said.

Berta tried to calm the situation. "I understand, Tina. But it's okay."

"We're leaving," my mother said.

———

The sound of ocean waves crashing against the Grecian coast gains our dog's attention. He huffs out a quiet bark and tilts his head at the sound of the water. He approaches the TV and plants his front paws on the edge of the wooden television stand. Ashlynn and I laugh.

"I'm going to video him," I say. His nubby tail twitches with delight.

———

Remaining blissfully ignorant of a parent's trauma, like in *Mamma Mia*, was not an option for my brother and me. Our mother claimed bragging rights to everything that happened—whether it was her pain or someone else's.

"The worst thing that could happen is you could die. And you didn't die, so you're fine," Mom would say.

Her badges of honor were not on colorful metal bars. Her victories in battle were not lined up and displayed on her chest. Instead, she revealed her injuries in the subtle way the corners of her eyes would turn down, in her silence, or the forceful release of air from her lungs caused by the weight of her thoughts. Can't you see them? Can't you hear her pain screaming into your ears? I can.

She waited for someone to see her pain. Someone to know and understand. She waited for someone to hear what her movements, silences, tears, emotionless stories, and glances were saying. She wanted a man to save her. She wanted someone to wrap her in the most loving embrace a human could offer and never let go.

I fear she knew that not dying didn't mean she had survived. Living and breathing the pain of the past isn't survival. And worse, surviving is not healing. But I get it. That was her way of making sense of a world that was so brutal that a slow death by anger, addiction, and jealousy was an actuality. And, when she would say it, I would feel less scared. Even though it was a lie, it gave me a small amount of hope that she was okay.

My mother shared her stories of the life she knew—lives,

relationships, and innocence lost to distrust, hate, and alcohol. Like the simple way she'd describe her father pointing a shotgun to her mother's face threatening to kill her in front of her eyes—a memory she shared void of fear and sadness. She knew that as long as it wasn't death, it was better.

I believe that to be a true victor in the battles against the history of abusive trauma at the hands of those who promised to love me, I must not inherit the behavior. And though I know I shouldn't brag about my battle scars, sometimes, very rarely, I do. I do because it gives me power over them—for a brief moment. However, the moment is short-lived, and I regret allowing the words to exit my mouth. I wish I could un-tell the story and hide it back inside of me.

The stories aren't where I should place my focus. How I felt and what they did to me is what needs to be heard and healed.

My mother and father became used to the daily injuries inflicted by powers more significant than their own and by out-of-control mental illness and addiction. My mother, too, was a collector. She collected moments of horror as trophies—awards for the many battles she and my father, whether together or apart, had endured and lived to tell.

She had a way of getting on with life, continuing to do everyday things. A lover's lousy behavior often interrupted her routine with hours of howling cries from her bedroom while I held my breath until she stopped. She never saw the panic her crying caused me. She never understood the pain that spread throughout my body and the tightness in my chest. Because as soon as she would stop crying, I wanted her to move forward—heal. And I knew my pain was my own and would never be more important than hers.

Instead of choosing better or moving out of the routine of people that would constantly hurt her, Mom stayed focused inside the trauma. She committed to her story line because it became proof of her obsession that horror was the norm. And her trauma filled life became her gold metal.

She loved the shock value in the stories of her history; and my mother was sure she had earned the right to brag. In contrast to my friend's family, she had unique strengths that she would keenly make you aware of. For example, an average mother may be able to run a mile in under eight minutes, but my mother could wake up the day after finding her lover with another and make the best cup of coffee you've ever had. She could play jump rope with her two younger siblings while her father berated her mother and accused her of having another man's child. She could take her younger sister's hand to pull her to safety, away from the fistfight erupting in the kitchen, or remain calm through her sobs and go about her week while the father of her children was missing on an alcoholic bender. Not only that, she could take you into a made-up world to distract you from an awful truth.

My mother's stories became her battle scars. She would tell them with pride relaying them in such a way that you would think they didn't hurt her. As if she was immune to their heartbreak. She cried in solitude with her children, yet she expected the world to know she was in pain. Our mother ached for love and safety but never knew how to find it; she was never able to live her happiest life. Not one single moment was sufficient to heal her pain and sadness.

Her fear of being alone was suffocating. And what she endured in the past was inevitable to happen again in her future. Intimacy laced with intoxication and toxic intensity was the only kind she knew. Her sadness was always present. Her longing for adoration from the wrong type of men was constant.

My mother was a deeply feeling beautiful soul whose heart was so large that it constantly needed to be filled with love. She knew she couldn't trust the people around her with the task. Soon, her heart was so fractured that all attempts at mending it failed.

There was never a moment when she didn't long for someone to love her above all else. Above other women, above money, friends, addiction, and lust. She ached for the safety of pure unconditional love from the day she was born until the day she died. Like the type of love I've yearned for—but I have outgrown the chance for that kind of love from my parents. I have given up on finding this sort of love from anywhere else but within myself. My healing calls for me to love myself.

And let me tell you about my father in the words of my mother—the legendary Tarzan. My father can get up so early that by the time you climb out of bed, he would have already survived a motorcycle crash and a gunshot wound, then burned down the house of the person who ran over his mother with a car, drank a pot of coffee, and smoked a pack of cigarettes. By noon, ten women would have fallen in love with him and, more often than not, had their hearts broken.

Like my father, I do not wear my wounds openly. We hide them inside ourselves, where no one else can see. We behave as if we're stronger than we are, and we judge those who show weakness. We pretend we don't need a shoulder to lean on— after all, we never had one. We see the unfair nature of the world through a lens lacking of optimism and hope. Like my father, I know that no one is worried about anything but themselves. Our pain is irrelevant. Mom also told Dad's stories without his permission, and his were tales of the worst kind. He was and is a silent warrior. He was born into a hell I cannot imagine. What I've already relayed was only part of his history—the rest is too evil to repeat in words. I will respect his oath of silence for those horrors and allow his bulletproof armor to protect him.

My father has a particular kind of strength endowed to few—one that's difficult to describe but you can feel it on a visceral level. He possesses a persistent and tenacious sort of strength that allowed him to persevere through his past. But not without daily torture from the demons residing in his soul. He accepts responsibility for his actions and admits regret. He is a rare masterpiece of a human being, and so was my mother.

I love you, Dad. I know you loved Mom and still do. I miss her. I love her. But, now I'm angry. Angry that she never learned to heal. Mad that no matter how hard I tried, I was never enough. Mad that neither myself nor my brother was ever first for either of you. We weren't even second. I know neither of you ever felt safe; how could you possibly feel happiness?

And although I'm mad as hell, I understand.

———

The song "Super Trouper" erupts from the television. Ashlynn and I leap to the floor again, wiggling our hips while we sing.

"Tonight, the super trouper lights are gonna find me, shining like the sun (sup-p-per troup-p-per)."

Chapter Ten

The Turntable

Ashlynn and I spend as much time together as possible during this summer. It has been short and fast. We find ourselves preparing for her next phase of life—an apartment off-campus and shopping for back-to-school supplies.

Ashlynn will be entering her sophomore year of college. She's narrowed her field of study to psychology and sociology. Her interest in those subjects is the result of her life experience with her biological father—my first husband—and the therapist that helped her survive. If she can understand, then perhaps she can forgive him.

I left Ashlynn's father when she was two years old. Our divorce wasn't final until she was four. I married Billy when she was five.

If a person's mental illness could be graphed, Ashlynn's biological father would be off the charts. She had contact with him until age fifteen. She loved him, of course, but was hurt and tormented by him to the degree that she may never recover—like me.

Ashlynn's first year at college was an academic success. She landed herself on the dean's list both semesters. She went through middle school and high school absolute in her decision that she would not attend college. I didn't argue with her about it because I knew better. Instead, I'd say, "Okay, but while you're in high school, I want you to do everything you would need to do if you were planning on going to college." She agreed.

Ashlynn's list of back-to-school necessities is mostly made up of things she needs for her first apartment: curtains, a cutting board, a bath mat, and a blender. We visit Home Goods. Shopping must be an inheritable gene. Ashlynn and I both love it. We grab a cart and proceed to walk down each aisle at a pace that's slow enough to inspect every item on the cluttered shelves. Her list isn't too extensive; it's really more an excuse to "see what else they have."

I don't usually consider buying electronics at Home Goods, but today I think I might. We find a few dozen suitcase-style record players. The maker fashioned the outer shell to have the vintage look of a Samsonite suitcase. Brilliant. Of course we had to get one. At eighty-nine dollars, I thought it was a steal. Ashlynn chose one in a cheery peach color.

The built-in speaker is remarkably small. I tell Ashlynn, "You know, I had a record player in high school, and the speakers were half my height. I used them as bedside tables."

She laughs in disbelief. "No way. That's huge."

"That turntable from high school got left behind in Missouri. We ran out of room, and I had to leave it behind with my boyfriend."

"How long did you live in Missouri for again?" asks Ashlynn.

"A year and a half. The day after I graduated from high school, we came back to Maine."

"So you were a junior in high school when you moved there?"

"Yup."

She finds a new treasure and picks it up to examine it. "Oh, Mom, can I get this bowl for my popcorn popper? It's only six dollars."

"Yes, get it. That's a good price."

Ashlynn places the white glass bowl in the cart, smiling to herself with satisfaction. And I smile to myself as I think of Popcorn, our dog when we lived on Chase Street in South Portland, before we moved to Missouri.

———

When I was in eighth grade, my mother's diet expanded to air-popped popcorn. It swiftly became the favorite snack in our house. It smelled wonderful and felt a little health conscious. We even got a dog that we named Popcorn. He was an aggressive black-and-white, curly-haired Cocka-Poo Terrier: Cocker Spaniel, Poodle, and Terrier mix. We'd lived at Chase Street in South Portland for two years by then. I even had a best friend—Kim. It was a miracle.

Then, before freshman year, my best friend's parents sent her to a private school. I understand I had something to do with that decision. Of course, I'm sure I wasn't a parents' first choice for their child's best friend. I told horrible stories about my family and stole beer. My reputation had followed me. Even when I was younger, parents forbade their kids from playing with me. I assumed it was the legend of Tarzan. But, here in South Portland, there is no legend of Tarzan. Just me—loose-cannon, hyper, off the wall, troublemaking me.

I had never had anyone of my own before. But, finally, I had a best friend. Then she was gone, and I was alone again. Boys never wanted to be my boyfriend. I tried so hard, too. I ached with the desire to feel wanted. No one had ever adored me, and I imagined the feeling of being adored was beautiful.

After many low-level crushes, I landed my first big crush. Dean. Dean wasn't very nice to me, but I liked the way he looked. He was handsome in a bad boy kind of way, confident and charismatic like my dad.

I could tell he liked that I had a crush on him, and he kept it alive without a single ounce of commitment. Kim took him from me for a bit, which broke my heart. But, in the end— after a three-year crush—I was nothing to him, and I made myself move on. He took advantage of anything physical my immature and inexperienced self would offer him, then he'd ignore me, leaving me feeling humiliated and ashamed.

Aunt Berta lived with us for a while during this time on Chase Street in South Portland. It wad my bedroom that she shared. Berta was eighteen and began dating one of my friends, who was fourteen. He gave her his virginity. Their sex life became horrifically offensive and public. "We have a competition to see who can make the other the horniest," said Aunt Berta as she jerked him off under a blanket while sitting on the couch with myself, Casey, and at least two other friends. To make sure she would win the current wager, she put her head under the blanket.

My mother would sometimes intervene, saying, "Stop having sex in front of the kids, Berta."

I began not feeling so safe with Berta. She pitted family against me and would often go about life as if I didn't exist. I became emotionally afraid of her and deeply uncomfortable. I learned that she was not a keeper of secrets and whatever hell she had been through made her selfish and uptight. Berta's ability to injure the psyche of those around her became potent and infectious. She revealed a sexual sickness within our family that I had hoped to hide since moving to South Portland; she paraded it around my friend group freely ripening my shame.

And then it happened: I met a boy who was as love deprived as me. His name was Mark, and it was the summer before my junior year of high school. He was my first weighted blanket. Having him love me felt like the warm sun on my skin and the happiness of wrapping myself in a heavy blanket and resting all of my worries away on a comfortable couch. He and I became very close. We craved the close physical connection we shared. However, because neither of us knew ourselves very well, we didn't get to know each other very well.

———

Ashlynn and I make our way through Home Goods to look at the handbags. We share unique finds and discounted Michael Kors, but neither of us plans to buy one. We head to the long checkout line to pay for her purchases while I daydream.

———

My mother continued to date many men. Jon came back into the picture, and he lived with us for a while at Chase Street. Then one night, he never came home. My mother's howling began again. It had never entirely stopped after her New Jersey heartbreak. The sounds of her bellowing cries were a constant throughout all the years of my life with her, and I can still hear them ringing through my mind today.

Jon didn't come home because he had spent the night with another woman. My mother's sadness was unbearable. It consumed her. We could hear her from behind the locked doors of the bathroom and bedroom. Day and night. Mornings before school and in the evenings instead of dinner.

A few weeks later, he came by to collect his things. They "took a nap" that afternoon. It made me feel ashamed and confused.

During this period of my life, my mother stressed how I should be more like Kim—my recent and now gone best friend—how important being skinny was, and how she would punch me if I ever lied to her.

Being skinny and pretty was by far the number-one most

important thing to my mother. The second was having a relationship with a man. In her eyes, being skinny was equal to having power over my life as a whole. It made her proud of me. It was something that had been taken away from her when the unfortunate event of having two children so young occurred. So I had to do it for her. But not without the hypocrisy of her telling me, "You should be able to eat whatever you want." As if being skinny was a mind-over-matter miracle bestowed on the rare few who had an intolerance to calories.

So I didn't eat much and I exercised like crazy, committing myself to a sport every season of high school and filling my entire summers with swimming and track. I played field hockey in the fall, swimming in the winter, and track in the spring. Weather permitting, I ran home from any practice I could for extra exercise. I'd come home late at night after being out with my friends, and I would go for a midnight run before bed.

And again, my hypocritical mother would admonish me by repeating, "You shouldn't run, Tina. Have you ever seen a runner in slow motion? Your body bounces with every stride. It's so ugly, and it's going to make your skin sag."

A few months later, my mother met her second husband. His name, like my boyfriend, was also Mark. He was in the Navy and ten years younger than her. They got married when I was seventeen, he was twenty-three, and my mother was thirty-three.

He was the reason we moved to Missouri. Even though I was captivated with my own Mark, my first young love, I was a solid swimmer on the swim team, and Casey had friends— it was not easy for him to make friends. She still tore us, yet again, from a place we wanted to be our home, and relocated us for her man.

We drove two vehicles, packed with our cheap belongings and my stolen wardrobe, thirty-one hours to reach Fulton, Missouri.

Yes, I said stolen wardrobe. Being a poor kid in high school is brutal. Add not being able to afford what's in style, and I felt like even more of an outcast. A friend taught me how to steal. I was good at it, and I filled my closet in no time. Then the friend got caught, so I stopped out of fear.

It was November of 1987. High school midterms had just ended, and I would be starting the second half of my junior year in a town so far from the ocean and mountains that it changed me.

We drove straight to Mark's mother's house. Of course. Where else would a twenty-three-year-old just out of the Navy go?

We lived there long enough for us to end up back on food stamps. My brother and I slept in the tiny crawlspace of an attic where we couldn't even stand up. Mark's younger brother, Jeff, was my age. He tried to have his way with me. I was too weak and broken to resist him.

My mother tore me from the comforting weight that my Mark's love blanketed me with when we moved to Missouri. He missed me and loved me. I was shattered by our separation too, so I pulled myself away from him and became cruel.

I loved him. Again, survival took center stage. I crushed him, and I don't blame him for spreading rumors about me after I left. Everyone I knew in South Portland already loved to hate me.

My mother was the first to find a job in Fulton. She became a receptionist at a dental office. Weeks later, her husband, Mark, found a job too. Both of them finding jobs financed the move out of his mother's house and into a rental across town.

It was clear from the moment we arrived in Missouri that we should not have come. Tensions were high, and all of us were very unhappy. I sensed that Mark no longer loved my mother. He wanted to move on with his life without us. Why would a twenty-three-year-old man wish to be a stepfather to two teenage kids? All conversations between Mark, my brother, and I ceased. And yet, we tried to make a life in Fulton, Missouri.

My mother and I joined a gym. The owner, Randy, became friends with my mother. We visited his home one evening while his wife and three-year-old son were asleep in their bedrooms, and the three of us drank beer.

Randy led me into the dark kitchen, where he could approach me alone. Randy came on to me. He kissed me and pressed my hands over his erection and tried to persuade me to take a shower with him. He pushed his body against mine while my drunk mother was passed out on his couch, his wife was footsteps away, and their three-year-old son, who I had babysat often, was in the next room. His hands roamed over my body. I fled. I never told my mother, and I never went back to the gym.

The only other occasions I can recall a man touching me without my consent were the dozens of times I got felt up at music concerts. It was like getting fingered over my pants from behind when I pushed through the crowd. And as soon as it would happen, I would turn around to the group to identify the creepy perpetrator, but instead, all the faces I could see were pointed toward the band. I never knew who committed the vile feel-ups.

After a couple of months in Missouri with no friends, a wonderful girl named Pamela befriended me. She saved me from going to the library instead of lunch every day—I'd go through each day with no food because going to the lunchroom alone was terrifying. And eating wasn't a priority. Food wasn't always available, and neither was the money to buy it anyway.

Pamela welcomed me into her home for days at a time. I spent the holidays with her. I fled my home, my brother, and my mother to be with her, and she welcomed me into her world. She was kind and sweet and so generous with her life. And of course, in the end, I was cruel to her too. I became confident after meeting more friends, and so I started mistreating Pamela. Pam, I'm sorry. I didn't know how to be better.

Through Pam, I met another boy named Mark. He was controlling and jealous, but it felt so good to be wanted. The relationship with him was like the heavy blanket of love had returned, and it was keeping me safe.

He went with me to buy the turntable. The stereo had a tall glass storage case that was taller than the three-foot speakers. Not only did it have a record player on the top, but it also had a radio and double cassette player. It was dark black with red lights that bounced, measuring the beat of the music. The stereo was my first significant purchase. I was proud of it.

During my senior year, after dating Mark for a year out of the year and a half we were in Missouri, I grew tired of his controlling behavior and broke up with him. He threatened suicide. My mother befriended him and allowed him into our home, where he could beg for me to take him back, threaten suicide, and plead his way back into my favor.

I was trapped; it felt like it was never going to end. And my mother was helping him when I needed her to help me. I became angry and felt as if my mother was strangling me with his nearness and her inability to protect me. I cannot count how many days after our breakup that I would come home from school to find him in our living room with her, and I reacted by kicking his legs and punching his face. I remember I would slap his chest and face and scream, "Get out of my house and leave me alone."

"Tina, he's sick. He's suicidal. Just let him talk to you," my mother repeated daily.

I fled.

One day he went into the woods and shot himself in the thigh. "I did it for you," he said from his hospital bed.

He survived. I took him back.

My mother and her Mark got a divorce.

I drowned out their arguments by blasting music out of the tall speakers attached to the turntable next to my bed. I coped by ignoring my mother and her immature husband. My brother couldn't cope with our situation.

He went missing. My mother spotted him through a window of the Fulton McDonald's. He was alone, and he was crying. My brother sank into a deep depression and left Missouri, going to live with our father who was temporarily residing in Florida. From that decision forward, Casey was shamed by our mother for leaving her, flooding and drowning him with guilt. I was proud of him. He did something for himself; something that I and neither of our parents could do. It was brave and it was the right thing to do.

I remained in Missouri with our mother, alone.

Casey and Mark had both left her. And so had countless men before them.

She sprawled herself over the floor and howled. A cannonball punched my chest. I wanted to yell and scream at her. I wanted to punch and kick her. I hated her. But I couldn't. I loved her. And we were alone.

This time I didn't hide or flee. Instead, I sat on the floor beside her, put her head in my lap, and let her cry. For the first time, I embraced her while she wept. I had always been too afraid before. But today, I knew she needed me. I pulled her tear-soaked hair out of her face and caressed it back over her ear.

I absorbed the earth-shattering sounds of her sobs. My heart pounded so hard and so fast that my ribs threatened to break into tiny pieces. Anxiety pushed against all of my muscles, but I refused to let it make me run away. I stayed with her and shared her pain. My throat ached with fear and my gut burned with heat. The outside world became irrelevant.

"Let's move your bedroom downstairs into Casey's old room. Then you and I will be next to each other," I suggested. She nodded her head against my lap once while I patted her hair. Her sadness turned her mouth down so far I didn't recognize her. She wept for what felt like hours. My pants were soaked with her tears, snot, and saliva.

The whole day passed before she began to show signs of life. The sun was starting to set, and the outside world was darkening. I needed her to move forward and out of her pain. I needed her to heal. I opened the stereo cover containing the turntable and turned on the radio—a local pop radio station played "November Rain" by Guns N' Roses.

I held her hand and led her to the bedroom she'd shared with Mark on the house's second floor, the only room up there. We carried each piece of furniture and clothing down the narrow stairs and filled Casey's old room with her things. We became roommates in a tiny house in a town called Fulton.

"Let's move back to Maine, Mom."

And we did. With the help of my father and grandparents, the day after I graduated from high school, we loaded a pickup truck full of our things, minus the turntable that wouldn't fit, and returned to Maine. It was 1989. I was eighteen; my mother was thirty-four.

———

The clerk at checkout number six announces her availability. We push our cart over to her, as instructed, and Ashlynn unloads our treasures onto the counter.

"Oh, cool record player," says the clerk.

"Thank you," says Ashlynn with pride.

The clerk studies the box containing the turntable. "I didn't know we had these."

"There's a bunch left," says Ashlynn. "You should grab one before they're gone."

"I will." The clerk inserts the box into a giant shopping bag and hands it to Ashlynn then finishes ringing up the rest of our items, and I pay.

We drive home by way of the familiar route over Tukey's Bridge in Portland. To this day, a full thirty years later, every time I go this route, I think of my return to Maine from Missouri and my first trip back over Tukey's Bridge.

———

The moment we reached Portland, Maine, I rolled down all of the windows in my car. I'd spent the last twenty-eight hours driving with my Chow Chow puppy, Mica, and our elderly cat, Kitty. They, too, perked up as soon as the fresh air began moving through the car.

I became aware of the smell of the ocean. This moment became forever seared into my mind as one of my favorites in life—the moment when I could smell the sea again.

The sweet, savory, salty smell filled my malnourished soul with a vitamin that I had been starving for. It made me cry. I never knew it smelled so beautiful. I must have been used to it before we moved away. Coming back provided me with an awareness of its existence and more, an appreciation and love for where it came from: the ocean. The pine trees that accented the sea, the fields, and rivers—all a bouquet I didn't know that I was in love with.

My father had prepared an apartment for my mother in Trenton, which we reached three hours later. It was another new place, but at least it was Maine. I felt like I was home.

———

Ashlynn and I drive in silence with our windows open, and the smell of the ocean makes me smile.

"You've been quiet, Mom. Is everything okay?"

"Absolutely, sweet girl." I place my palm over her hand. "I love you," I say.

"I love you too, Mamma."

"Before you go back to school, we'll go get you some new pajamas too," I say.

"Oh, yay. Thank you, Mom."

"I'm so proud of you, honey," I tell her. She smiles and puts her head on my shoulder while I drive. "Remember your to-do list this year. The first on your list is to study, the second is to have fun, but above all is to take care of yourself—rest, nutrition, and mindfulness."

"I know, Mamma."

———

I realize how easy it would have been for me not to have gone to college and how tragic that would have been. If I had given in to all of the inconsistencies of my parents and if I had admitted my sense of self-worth matched theirs, I may not have.

It turns out I'm the only one in my immediate family who went to college. The institution of school wasn't a priority to my mother or my father. Both were high school dropouts with little desire for an education.

I recall a conversation with my mother during one of my visits home during a college break. I was in my sophomore year of dental hygiene school. I studied hard and, for the most part, enjoyed the college experience. It was much better than high school. I remained underfed and over-exercised, but I loved the education and was proud of my accomplishments there.

During this particular trip home, my brother told my mother and me about a high school friend who became a stripper in a big city, and while she was stripping, she met and began dating a famous football player. My mother was so impressed that this girl's stripping talents had landed her a professional football player.

"Just think, Tina," said my mother, "that could have been you." These words have replayed in my mind over and over ever since that day.

I sank into a pit of defeat at her words, and every time I recall it since. I was speechless and unable to argue that my education was a much better choice than stripping. Or perhaps posing for *Playboy* as my mother had always hoped I would do.

She kept a foot-and-a-half-tall stack of *Playgirl* magazines in the trailer for all to see. But she was sure there was something wrong with Casey because he stole a picture of a woman's vagina from an unlocked vehicle on our street. The hell she put him through for it was extreme. The only normal behavior in the situation was his.

Another moment of hypocritical anguish occurred when Mom thought celebrating New Year's Eve 1991 with my college friends and me was normal. She danced with one of my male classmates and kissed him at midnight. That was the night I had my first adult panic attack.

I didn't understand that it was a panic attack then, but I know it well now. Doom spanned my chest. My gut felt sickened and bottomless. The thought of my future life began strangling me with fear. I couldn't speak, laugh, or smile. I remember my eyes widened and my breathing became shallow. I held onto the railing as people danced below me. I was frozen and confused. The crowd went on with their night and rejoiced around me, celebrating the new year. I couldn't move.

Chapter Eleven

Layers of an Antique Couch

I make a cup of hot tea in a clear glass mug, dipping the tea bag in and out of the steaming liquid. A cloud stained the color of cherry oak swirls and darkens the water.

"Did you pack your extra contacts, Ashlynn?" I ask.

"Yes. And I've got enough solution for about a week. I plan on going grocery shopping with my roommates tonight, though. I'll pick some up."

"Okay, great. Do you have your medications?"

"Yes."

"Okay, well, if you've forgotten anything, I can mail it to you."

"Thanks, Mom."

"I'm excited for you, Ashlynn. I'm also going to miss you so much. I think I'll have to visit soon." I squeeze Ashlynn in a tight hug.

"Oh yes. We can have lunch at The Fork and Spoon. They have great vegan options."

"I would love that." I pull away and smile at her. "I'm so glad we packed the truck last night."

"Ugh, me too."

"There is no student body to help us move you in this year, though. How many flights of stairs is it?"

"Just one." Ashlynn smiles.

Billy enters, wrapping his watch around his wrist. "Ready to go, girls?"

"Ready," Ashlynn moves toward the door.

She has her plants seat belted into her passenger seat and we follow her car in our truck. Two hours later, we move Ashlynn into her first apartment near UMO—the University of Maine in Orono, which is the party school capital of the state. But I don't worry about Ashlynn partying too much. She will thrive and make much better decisions than I did in college and, since she has started eating a plant-based vegan diet, she is much more careful about what she puts in her body.

Once she's all moved in, I delay leaving. One of my biggest fears as a mother is that Ashlynn may need me, and I won't be there. Like when I left her father. When she was with him, and I wasn't there. It scared the hell out of me. I worried she would feel abandoned, or worse, that she would think I didn't love her.

I can sense awkward energy in the apartment. Ashlynn wants to begin her life at college, but she is far too polite to say so. I know her so well. I need to give her space so she can flourish.

"If you need anything, please call, honey," I say, extending my embrace.

"I will, Mom. I love you."

"I love you too."

"Give me a hug, Ashlynn," Billy says. He wraps his arms around her shoulders and squeezes her tight.

We exit the complex of apartments, and I feel an emptiness that only an indulgent and overprotective helicopter parent of a grown child going off to college knows. I am proud, worried, excited, and sad.

My phone lights up. I've received a text. *Hey, Tina, it's Amy. You know your mom's loveseat that you gave me after she died? Do you want it back? I'm never going to re-cover it, and I don't have space to store it anymore.*

Sure, I'll take it back. I have the room now. I'd love to re-cover it.

Next time you come up, let me know. I'll meet you.

We're in the area now. Can we swing by and pick it up? We have Billy's truck.

Yes, I'll meet you in Ellsworth. In front of Marden's. Okay?

Perfect. Leaving Orono now. See you in about an hour.

Billy isn't thrilled about the extra driving time but he agrees. Our drive toward Ellsworth is silent. Amy is the mother of my brother's first child, Carley. Leaving Ashlynn at school and picking up Mom's couch leads me to think of my brother, Casey.

Casey is a tortured soul. He has been sad most of his life, so he's spent most of it under the influence of something. As soon as he became an addict, I became afraid of him. In my experience, addiction changes people.

The first of his four or five thirty-day rehab stays was when I was in my freshman year of college. Rehab forced our mother and father to pay attention to him. It forced them to spend time with him. If only they had been that focused on my brother throughout his whole life, things might have turned out different for him. I drove from Westbrook College in Portland, where I was studying dental hygiene, to Bangor, where Casey was learning about sobriety. We met once per week while he was there.

At the first meeting, the family counselor told us to do something that I was afraid to do: share with Casey, my mother, and my father one thing about each of them or their behavior that upset me. Just like when my dad was in rehab, I had nothing to say. I blamed a test in pharmacology for missing that particular day. I thought I was in the clear. But I wasn't.

Our counselor made me make up for what I had missed. I hadn't prepared anything to say because I thought I was off the hook. I hated this part. How could I find something to say that wouldn't come back to haunt me with my mother, that wouldn't hurt my brother, and that wouldn't push my father further away?

I decided on religion for my mother. I knew she would not give a shit about God. She wouldn't be insulted if I said that I wished she'd focused on religion in our lives. I knew she thought it was all bullshit anyway. There was no way she could have lived the life she lived if there was a God. And I sort of felt the same way.

We were not good enough for God.

We were not the kind of people that went to church. And

if we did—which was rare and only ever happened when a friend invited us—we stood out like sore thumbs. We didn't belong, and I was sure everyone could see it.

I told my father that I didn't like how wishy-washy he was. I said that because it's what my mother said about him. When he said he would do something, it sometimes took him forever to do it.

And I told my brother I wanted to be able to come into his bedroom and jump on his bed and hang out with him.

There were no ruffled feathers from any of it. I survived.

But now, I was scared of Casey. I didn't trust addiction. It made people do things out of desperation regardless of the risk of injury. He became isolated and volatile. His sadness had turned to anger, and I feared it. His moods were unpredictable, and I could see that he was often on the verge of losing his composure. He became fearless. He would become so overly intoxicated that I thought he would overdose. He took enormous risks while driving, and his overconfidence in his ability to operate machinery, four-wheelers, or motorbikes scared the hell out of me. But I still loved him even though I was angry at him for doing the exact things he hated in our parents.

He played and lost the dangerous game of Russian roulette with drugs, and the addiction switch got flipped. He has struggled his entire life, self-medicating with narcotics and alcohol to treat his depression and bipolar disorder, along with anxiety and panic disorders. Our mother also suggested

Casey might have schizophrenia since we had relatives with the disease.

Our mother told him he was disabled. She told him that the drugs would win, and he was powerless to resist their torment, infusing his mind with the helpless notion that addiction was a war he was destined to lose. She didn't see how strong he was and always has been. She didn't see what he was capable of because she only knew a life riddled with addiction, so in her eyes, it was a certainty for him too. And so, he remains defeated.

Within a year of my mother's death, my brother became hospitalized for a systemic blood infection that stemmed from his favorite needle site. I was too scared to visit him. Thank God he survived.

———

Billy and I approach the Ellsworth McDonald's and turn in to Marden's parking lot behind it. I spot the love seat in the back of Amy's navy-blue pickup truck. We transfer the couch to Billy's truck, then three hours later, we return home with an unexpected gift: a burnt-orange artifact heavy with dust and stuffing so old it had turned to sand. My mother had told everyone she wanted to get it reupholstered. Someone had to do it.

It would be me.

The love seat wasn't originally my mother's. My mother's belongings had consisted of mismatched hand-me-downs.

Her vanity used to be mine, her television couch was her father's who picked it up along the side of the road, her bedroom set came from a yard sale, and her entertainment center from Service Merchandise. She owned neither Davis nor Henderson family heirlooms, except for a tin full of buttons that belonged to my father's mother. Her knickknacks were a collection of yard sale finds that wouldn't even resell at the estate sale after her death.

The only thing she kept and carried with her throughout her life were the love letters and cards she'd received from friends, relatives, and the men she dated. Some letters dated back to the 1970s, and some of her scribbles and artwork were from the 1960s. She kept them throughout all the years of her life, ever since the first romance. Boxes, filled with paper remembrances, have traveled with her from town to town, state to state, and home to home. Her collection of letters was evidence of her heartbreaks and clues toward solving the mystery of her unhappiness.

After her death, Billy, Ashlynn, and I decided that these letters needed a cremation ceremony too. I wanted to pay some sort of tribute to these letters that had meant so much to her. So we built a backyard bonfire, then each one of us took a piece of paper from her keepsake boxes and held it for a few seconds before tossing it into the hot flames and repeating the process with the next letter. I was relieved not to find the New Jersey heartbreak letter, but I was a little worried about what Ashlynn might read every time she unfolded a note. I suggested we not read anything because they were my mother's secrets. Ashlynn understood.

My mother's other most cherished possessions were her clothes. They had grown out of style, and many were mended and altered to fit her. She had filled all four closets and all four bureaus in her tiny condo—the second home she'd ever purchased.

This love seat came from her first boss after moving from Trenton to Portland in 1994. He committed suicide in 2000.

After his family took everything they wanted from his estate, they invited my mother—his secretary and enabler—to take what she wanted. I was pregnant with Ashlynn and nearly thirty years old at the time. My mother was forty-five. Her boss's death furnished her with a dark green velour antique couch, the burnt-orange love seat, a dining room table, and an oriental rug.

She would brag, "He's the city's leading neurologist. Brilliant but suffering and mad. A drug addict." She was impressed with this. "He passes out between patients. He sleeps in his office and keeps his patients waiting hours to see him. They think he's just busy." His patients had life-or-death issues and fears they prayed he could help them with, and he could barely keep his eyes open.

"His ex-wife, Christine, is so jealous of me. She knows he wants me," my mother would say. I am still trying to understand why she believed every man she encountered wanted to have sex with her. What was the reason? I'm almost positive no man has ever said no to having sex with her. She let me know every time she had sex. Maybe not always with words, but she made it clear. By her noises, by her messy bed afterward, the redness in her cheeks. She never hid it.

———

This love seat needed a fresh start. It would be a significant undertaking. The labor would be great, and yet in the process, I would find comfort. It became a symbol of welcoming her back into my home even though she'd pissed me off so many times. Even though I hated her, I loved and missed her.

I knew I would discover what this love seat—this symbol of my mother's carnage—meant to me. The process of its restoration would allow me to recover and replace memories as they present themselves along the way. What kind of resolution will it bring? How will the couch's repurposing impact me and my healing? I wonder.

My stomach flutters with anticipation of the unknown. The resurrection of stories will unfold, and, in the end, I will have closure.

A few weeks later, I begin its restoration—my first of many reupholstering projects. I have no idea how to start. I watch one YouTube video of the process—the number one thing I learned is that the furniture is my teacher. Study it. Take it apart one section at a time and hold on to the pieces of material—they are my blueprints. Replace each section of fabric in reverse.

I caress the outside edge of the dirtied burnt-orange fabric.

It had aged so much that some areas appear blackened and decayed. I discover a seam on the back—this will be the first to come off and the last to be replaced.

I'm curious about its history. How many layers will I find? What colors and patterns will I discover? I begin peeling away its flesh. My body feels solid and calm, and I breathe in and out with a regular rhythm. I remove each tack, nail, and staple with force and precision.

The focus and repetition required by this task is my therapy.

Like writing, the quiet and repetitive nature of plucking out each tack followed by peeling back the layers of history within this couch settles my fears—this is my safe place. Alone. The place I have gone whenever no one was there to comfort me. Comfort was up to me. Even when my mother was in the room, I was still alone. When rage engulfed our home, I ran to hide. Alone. When she looked through me as if I didn't exist, I was alone.

Alone is where I can breathe and think and where I know, without a doubt, that I am okay.

Under the orange mask, I find a dark red velour. Its deep bloodied hue strikes me as beautiful yet angry. The fabric is torn, but not from wear and tear—it had an injury caused by trauma. As if someone had stabbed her with a knife, then it ripped across her bosom. What had happened?

I brush away particles of dirt and frayed pieces of burnt orange. Someone covered her injuries. I'm angered by her past mistreatment, so I commit myself to repairing her wounds.

I will do more than cover them up. I won't ignore her pain. I will hold her like Ashlynn when she was injured and cradle her fears in my arms. I can be gentle and loving with this couch. Like I want to be with myself.

I chuckle. I remember a time before my love of collecting antiques—before I knew how to settle the traumatic infections festering within my soul. A time when I was wrapped so tight with self-inflicted restraints, I swear I could have exploded. Back when I covered up my wounds, I became someone else, and I pretended they didn't exist. I spent my entire life wrapping rubber band after rubber band around the chaos within my mind, but it provided only temporary numbness. There were constant mountains of chaos looming across the landscape of my mind. And anxiety threatened to snap every goddamn rubber band I used to hold it in.

I showed the world only strength. A bold, extroverted force that sometimes made me an intolerable bully. I appeared unapologetic, volatile, and inconsiderate. I partied as hard as I could and got as drunk as I could before throwing it all up. It was all a bluff. I was seeking happiness and safety by pretending I had it.

I pluck out nail after nail. Minutes turn to hours, and this calming repetitive task produces pounds of metal—rusted fabric nails, tacks, and staples that had all pierced through the deep layers of tattered fabric and scarred wood.

I think about how I used to be. How trying to become an adult, a whole person, was so hard for me. My younger self thought that someday life would get easier. I had hoped and dreamed for it my entire childhood. When I realized it was never going to be more manageable, I became furious.

I was so angry, rigid, and mean for so long. I was over-exercised and underfed. I enforced my strict expectation of physical perfection. I busied myself with fundraisers, road races, the Mrs. Maine America pageant—thank God I won. If I hadn't, it would have sent me into a cocoon of failure.

The year I spent as Mrs. Maine, mimicking many surrounding years before my recovery, was a full fifty-two weeks of nonstop self-imposed over-scheduling: two triathlons per week, while training; two road races, which I directed; thirty-four weekends spent at various Mrs. Maine events; two princess tea parties for Habitat for Humanity; and a fashion show for March of Dimes. Not to mention my full-time job and shared custody with an abusive co-parent, on top of girl's nights out full of drinking and dancing, and endless hours and dollars spent on my physical appearance. None of which provided the bliss I thirsted for.

I was brimming with anxiety and so unhappy.

My current marriage, tormented by doubt and mistrust, was rocky. My ex-husband was a constant source of confirmation for my shortcomings and mistakes. I accepted my ex-husband's insults as truth—even when they were fabricated. I justified his malicious attempts at defaming me and my new husband's character because I thought I deserved it. After all, he knew me well and used that knowledge to make me suffer.

His hateful verbal attacks were the opposite of the way my

mother looked through me like a piece of glass. He was able to see me. He could see the real fractured me. He imparted me with a shattered sense of self, wallowing in failure and insignificance. I decided to make up for this; I needed to work harder, be more, and be better.

Alas, three years after being crowned Mrs. Maine America, I came to realize that I needed help. I knew I was ill, and I was not able to help myself. I couldn't manage everything that I was forcing on myself. I needed rest, I needed boundaries, and I needed to heal. But admitting I couldn't handle it all or giving something up felt like defeat. This acknowledgment began my recovery. I sought to find a remedy to my emotional terror, and I wanted it quick and painless.

"Ha. Yeah, right," I say to the couch.

This red layer of velour was my forty-three-year-old self—boiling red hot like a furnace. Fear and pain were ripping their way out of me in any way they could. Anxiety threatened to snap every rubber band I had wrapped tightly around myself.

I now think of this time in my life as the opposite of rock bottom. Instead of losing everything to alcoholism, I gained more than I could handle and wasn't slowing down.

My drug of choice was stress.

Was this the moment in Alcoholics Anonymous when the hero crashes? Was this my snapping moment that would lead me into failure?

With my stress fisted in my hands, I teetered on the cliff of the highest mountain of commitment and self-destruction. I had achieved and acquired many things. I project managed my life into one never-ending anxiety attack. I knew I could fall at any moment, and yet I could not let it go. I couldn't stop. I knew no other way.

I found a therapist.

I will never forget her. I still recall and count on many of her words today. And I will never forget how I felt when I began seeing her. I convinced myself that I had stretched every last one of my million rubber bands to their limit, and I would either break or snap into unhealthier behaviors. I had no chance on my own.

With needle-nose pliers, I wiggle out each nail. And with the repetitive task of removing each one, I remember:

———

"The first question I ask all of my new patients is always the same: How can I help you?" My new therapist's exotic accent pleases me. I have no idea where she's from, but I know for sure it isn't Maine. She's older than me, which gives me the sense that she's wiser than I am. Her dirty blonde hair curls softly around the middle of her neck in no particular style. She doesn't smile, which I like. She's serious and ready to take me on.

"I'm mad all of the time," I answer. "I feel rage toward everyone and everything, and I'm having a hard time controlling it. I hate—and I mean hate, despairingly hate—every second of every day. I feel like I'm boiling with anger. And if I'm not angry, I'm numb. When I'm numb, I feel nothing. I'm not sure which is worse. The only time I feel relief is when I'm with my daughter. She is my only happiness."

"Why?" asks the therapist.

"Because she's the only proof I have that I'm a good person." I release a long breath. "I absolutely despise being around all of the adults in my life, and unfortunately, that includes my husband. It's sharing space with them that is so hard. Being near him or anyone else makes me claustrophobic. Like I can't breathe. There is palpable energy within the shared space that feels like it's going to reach out and hurt me." My eyes dart from one corner of the ceiling to the other. I look at her and see that she's listening. I focus on the air above her and continue.

"I am immediately triggered to anger at the presence of him or anyone. All it takes is hearing them. Just the sounds of them being alive: breathing, chewing, walking, footsteps on the floor, and the vibration it causes. Most of the time, I want to punch people. I want to yell at my husband and tell him to go away forever. I have to close my eyes and attempt to meditate when sharing parts of the house with him or sharing space at work with my coworkers.

"My husband has become my punching bag. And he allows it. I am cruel with my words, and I threaten divorce. The only thing I feel is anger. I've become my abusive ex-husband.

"I cannot tolerate things like when he brushes his teeth, chews, sniffs his nose, anything human, to be honest. The nature of human beings sickens me. I've always felt that way toward myself, but now it's with everyone. Everything makes me feel anger, disgust, and the desire to be violent all of the time. I'm a raging bitch. I feel like I'm boiling and overflowing with hate but constricted and restricted with my mouth covered and my arms bound all at the same time."

"You are saying that noises cause you discomfort?" asks the therapist.

"Oh, hell yes. To the point that I feel like I'm going to explode or vomit."

"Tina, I can say with almost one hundred percent certainty that your discomfort from noises has nothing to do with your husband or coworkers. We will uncover the source of this discomfort, this hypersensitivity, eventually, but for now, please continue."

The fury I felt from the noises in my childhood rises in my stomach. In a matter of seconds, I hear them all at once. The yelling, the crying, my mother's moaning, her howls of sadness, my parents having sex, the snap of her underwear, and the sound of sloppy make-out sessions between my mother and her men. My ears ring. My face reddens, and I instantly know why noises cause me discomfort. The noises remind me that I am not alone in my safe place. People's blatant noise making and zero consideration of my hearing it proves their lack of acknowledgment of me. Noise is my trigger for that old feeling of irrelevance.

Is sensitivity to noise a strong enough phrase for how noises make me feel? At any moment, I could shatter.

I swallow it all back down, and I move on. "Additionally, for the last few years, I have hated intimacy of any kind. Hate it. The request of a kiss or more makes me feel suffocated and trapped. I do it anyway because I'm supposed to. And then I cry. The perfect marriage welcomes intimacy, right?" I don't allow her to answer. I'm sure I know the answer: yes.

"I have no idea what intimacy for the sake of love even means. All I know is a man expects his wife to perform with some regularity, and I do so with disgust raging through my body. It hasn't always been this way for me. When he and I met, our intimacy was passionate and marvelous. But slowly, my trust in him eroded, and now, here I am. I'm utterly miserable. I'm confused and pissed off. I have no room for any emotion other than anger.

"When we're apart, my edges soften, and I know I love him. I can easily remember why I fell in love with him, and I cherish how he made me feel back then. He loved me. He adored me. He found me beautiful and intelligent, and regardless of how ugly it got with my ex-husband, he remained valiantly by my side. I craved him, his smell, and his touch. We had so much fun together, and I loved his compassion for people, his passion for life, and his affectionate teddy bear hugs.

"Not only can I feel love for him when we're apart, but I even look forward to seeing him again. Until I see him again, when I feel like our space is too confining, and I feel so much intense irritation and frustration that I cannot tolerate it. There is an undefined expectation in the air that suffocates me. I have no space inside this body or mind for anything else. I am full of anger and hatred.

"He is kind and caring, and I appreciate all of his attempts to make my life better and to make my daughter's life better. A part of him is genuinely remarkable and part of him that is human, just like everyone else, and I hate it. I've taken him off the pedestal I placed him on when we first met, and I've lowered my impression of him to that of every other untrustworthy man. And honestly, he doesn't even know it. He thinks I'm just being mean, nitpicky, and can't handle imperfection. Maybe he's right. I'm sure whatever is wrong is exactly what I deserve.

"All I know is I hate feeling this way. I rehash every mistake he has ever made, almost like I'm still looking for the truth. My inner voice has convinced me of his infidelity. Even if he has never had sex with another woman—although I believe that no man can be faithful with one hundred-percent certainty—I have witnessed behavior in him that indicates a man who is unable to say no to a woman. He likes attention from women way too much. And that is infidelity. I can sense energy, a tenseness that is all too familiar to me. It's sexual tension. He cannot close himself off as unavailable.

"And yet, I question this feeling. Am I super aware of these things because I saw them so many times growing up? Am I able to detect the subtleties of unfaithfulness because I have so much insight into the behaviors? Or am I just paranoid and delusional because of what I've witnessed? Is it possible that he is, in fact, the caring human and doctor his friends and patients compliment him on being? Or does he have us all fooled? I don't want to be 'that wife,'" I say as I hold up my fingers and make air quotes. "The stupid wife who doesn't know she's getting cheated on all the time.

"Another thing about Billy that makes me unable to trust him is that he is vague, and he withholds information. He is so afraid of making me upset that he avoids pissing me off. He doesn't understand that by not being direct or by him only telling me what he thinks I want to hear, he pisses me off even more."

My voice is loud and firm. My lips are tight as I speak. These feelings have all been raging inside for a long time. Without stopping for a reaction from my brand-new therapist, I continue my rant.

"Beyond my husband, I struggle outside of the home. I can't handle the simplest irritations, like when a piece of my hair is out of place or something is in my way. Clutter, interruptions, noise, communication with others—all take me over the edge. If I am distracted in any way, I boil with irritation, and I try like hell to swim away from a looming panic attack. Casual small talk with anyone, including the people I work with, actually causes me physical pain.

"I can't even handle someone holding a door for me— even if I'm right behind them. I feel like yelling, 'LEAVE ME ALONE; let me walk at my own damn pace. I can open the fucking door by myself. It would be best if you didn't acknowledge me, and I don't think your gesture is considerate.'

"Even when I'm alone in the car, I'm percolating with anger. My road rage is monstrous. I get so impatient when driving that I actually have chest pain. I'm afraid I'm going to give myself a heart attack or crash my car.

"There are days when I feel like I will eventually have no control over what's going on inside me, and I will respond the way I feel—aggressive and with physical violence. If too many people ask me how I am or how my weekend was, I feel like punching them in the face or telling them it is none of their fucking business. I fantasize about doing physical violence. Why am I so angry? None of these people did anything to me."

My question is legitimate and heartfelt, but I leave no room for an answer, not at the moment anyway. I go on and on. I count long lists of all the things I detest on my fingers but I always run out of fingers, then clutch my fists and start again.

"I feel like I hate all adult human beings, including myself. I hate all of our imperfections and all of our weaknesses. I hate the way we smell, talk, act, age, get fat, get disgusting. If someone breathes near me, I hold my breath. I don't want to touch anything that the public touches. I can't tolerate hearing people make noise of any sort around me. Jesus.

"I work in healthcare, and I am having more than a tough time faking my compassion and my patience. Human nature is ugly and repetitive among everyone I work with, and I can't stand it.

"I am utterly disappointed with the reality of my life. I always thought someday it would get better. That I would feel a sense of peacefulness and love. I've been waiting for it to happen. There is no fantasy, no perfect, and I am so fucking mad about it.

"Ever since I was a little girl, I have been waiting to be loved. Loved in a way that lets me know with one hundred percent certainty that I matter, that I am worth staying faithful for, keeping secrets for, and standing up for. I've outgrown my chance at this type of love. I didn't get it from my parents, so I thought perhaps I could find it with a man. Nope. I'm shit out of luck in the love, happiness, and trust department.

"I am so unhappy," I articulate slowly. "I need to do something; I cannot live like this anymore." I stop, release my shoulders and exhale. I fold my hands, look at the therapist, and wait for her next question.

Chapter Twelve

Red Velour

I pull at the final upholstery nail holding the dark red fabric to the back of the love seat. I shake my head. "I was so stressed back then," I say to the couch. I move to the right armrest. With needle-nose pliers, I pull at the bottom edge of the fabric. I can loosen the corner while pulling out a few nails at the same time. "Cool." The sensation of satisfaction trickles down my back—the opposite of how I felt during my early months in therapy.

To this day, I continue to have moments of claustrophobia in the presence of other adults. If anyone gets too close to me, I feel like I can't breathe. My anxiety attacks are few but still occur; and are followed by a day or two of depression. The difference now is I can handle it—sort of. I know I'm not going to be injured in some way. And when I say injured, I don't just mean my physical body, but also my person—myself— the soul inside of this physical form.

I also know that I fell in love with my husband because he was, and is, the exact opposite of everything evil I experienced before him. This wonderful and free feeling he gave me attracted me to him, yet with time, I felt vulnerable and out of control. Although I know he adored me, I was confused by his lack of restrictions around me. I felt lost. And at the same time, it's the reason I was able to begin to heal.

He gave me the room I needed.

———

Those moments with my therapist were vital to who I am now. I remember the tightness in my chest. My firm upright and uptight posture. I crossed my legs tightly and limited the amount of movement I allowed myself. I felt rigid, so I became a statue. I quivered. My entire body shook with anxiety—an uncontrolled shivering that also made my words shake. I was erupting.

I sensed that my therapist was more than a little thrown—she was concerned and probably a bit irritated. She shifted in her seat, uncrossed her legs, then crossed the opposite one over the other. I studied her. I wanted answers, and I needed help. I needed to know if she was able to provide that, and I wondered what she thought of everything she'd just heard from me. I could have had all of the warning signs of a crazed person on the verge of committing an act of violence for all I knew, but it was still important to me that she understood that I am fearless and strong.

As scared as I was, I still maintained a mask of strength. I wanted to prove with my actions and words that I was strong. But I wasn't. I felt weak and fearful.

Her silence allowed me to continue. "I'm afraid I'm not

perfect because I want to be beautiful beyond measure, yet I was not born that way. My mother told me that being beautiful was crucial for success and happiness. But I'm so unhappy, I must not have been beautiful. Or rather, I must not be.

"Me being skinny always made my mother proud. So now, if anything on my body jiggles, I freak out. I can't share cake with my coworkers when they bring one in, and when it's my birthday, I panic. How can I say no to my own birthday cake?

"My mother would lead me across the beach to her male friends. 'I want them to see you,' she would say. 'Mr. Maine is here, C'mon, Tina. I want him to see you.' But on the other hand, every time she got drunk, she criticized me for not being more like Kim—my best friend through middle school. 'Why aren't you more confident like Kim? Kim is so popular, Tina, why aren't you?'

"Me, the way I was, was never enough. I complied with all of her unusual expectations in search of her love. I knew she loved me in her own way, but I wanted her to love me differently. I wanted to feel safe and protected. I didn't want my physical form to dictate my success the way she assured me it would.

"I really, really, really want to be happy and at peace with my life, and with myself, yet I am so far from that, I'm not sure it's even possible for me." It was difficult for me to divulge my weaknesses because I still believed that I needed her to know she wasn't dealing with just any woman. I have been through hell. And if this therapist couldn't help me, I would swallow this pain and soldier on, like always. I worried that I might kill my husband or take my daughter and run away, but I knew I'd survive.

———

I catch a glimpse of the next layer of fabric under the red velour. It's dark green with alternating lighter green vertical stripes and tiny pink roses with green leaves.

I laugh out loud at the vision of my uptight self sitting on the way-too-fluffy couch with a woman I didn't even know; my knees pressed so tight together that I caused myself pain and had sore muscles the next day. I clasped my hands across my lap with my fingers so tight my knuckles turned white. A hair tie held my fine, bleached blonde hair back from my face with layers of hairspray containing it in place. "God, I was uptight. I was so stupid."

I remember the fitted navy-blue pencil skirt and matching blazer I wore that day. The tight white patent leather pumps turned my big toes in so far that the bones of my feet ached. Of course, I ignored the pain. I forced myself to always be in high heels. I squeezed my feet into shoes so snug and tall that I considered it exercise. It became clear that my immaculate personal presentation was one of my attempts to control and reach some perceived sense of perfection—more rubber bands.

Looking like you have it all together does not mean you do. In fact, for me, it was undeniable proof that I was struggling. Not only did I strive to look like I had it all together, but I tried to be sexy. I pushed intimacy away during this time of my life, but I still attempted to appear sexy. Why? How does that happen?

I had so many unbroken bad habits.

I was neat to the level of being a neat freak, controlling in personal relationships, strict with my diet and exercise, very competitive, envious of my happy friends, and, without a doubt, totally insecure. I was miserable.

I earned love by being beautiful, and men only wanted sex. Right, Mom? What else did I have to offer? I was pretty sure I had nothing to give that would make a difference in anyone's life, let alone my own.

———

Though not a deliberate sanctum, my mother's love seat absorbs these memories into its form. Dust floats into the air as I peel back the red fabric. I sneeze. Deciding to check the wooden frame for sturdiness, I grasp the hand-carved wooden armrest and give it a shake. Solid. The frame is solid. That's all that matters.

Who was I on the inside back then, before I started my recovery? Was I solid? Hell, no. A human being with a stable foundation doesn't mount layer after layer of masks and self-modifications: heavy makeup, three different breast augmentation surgeries, ear cartilage reduction, other body-altering surgeries that I won't mention, fake hair color, fake nails, hours in tanning beds, restrictive eating, over-exercising, and behavior contrary to what I respect in others. I did all of this and more but hated the attention I received from it.

This volatile stress hidden under my skin took its toll. My hair began falling out.

I pull away red velour and let the past go. "I was not stupid. I was struggling," I say to myself.

I place another piece of the red fabric in the pile that has accumulated on the floor. This pile of injuries has become round and heaping. I scoop it all up and present each tattered moment in the life of this love seat to the flames of the wood stove.

I had not dealt with a single one of my injuries. I delivered them all to my therapist in the form that I had become—a heaping pile of chaos and anxiety running on stress and starvation. I placed all of my hope for emotional tranquility into this woman.

Chapter Thirteen

A Rose Garden on Forest Green and Valentine's Day

I stroke the layer of green material, following the direction of its decorative lines. This fabric, like a garden, is calming. I smile at it. I did eventually find calm within myself. It took years of being mindful of my injuries.

As I begin removing the final layer from the love seat, I recall my therapist's words. "It can take years to help someone get a handle on past trauma, anger management, and obsessive tendencies. I need to know just how dangerous your situation is." She let out a long breath. "How long have you been feeling like this?"

"Since my first marriage ended in 2005. It worsened when my second marriage began about eight years ago, but even worse still since my mother died. That was less than two years ago. She was fifty-seven." With the declaration of my mother's age, I looked into the therapist's eyes with a level stare. This one statement said so much more, and I hoped she understood.

"And how old were you when your mother died?"

"Forty-one."

"Your mother was young."

"Yes."

"She was sixteen when you were born?"

"Yes."

"Having a child at such a young age, while still a child herself is evidence of a potentially tough upbringing. For you both."

"You could say that." Again, I hoped she was smart enough to understand my meaning. "She was fifteen when she got pregnant with me. I know she was sexually active well before that, though."

"Was there any substance use by her?"

"She began smoking cigarettes and drinking alcohol pretty young. I have a photo of her on her and my dad's wedding day. They were in my grandparents' kitchen. She was wearing a mini-wedding maternity dress; she was pregnant with me, holding a bottle of booze to her mouth and a cigarette in the other hand."

"Becoming sexually active at such a young age could indicate that your mother became stunted in sexual and intellectual maturity. The drinking, too, would have had an impact on this."

I look down at my crossed hands. My fingers squeeze each other. "Yeah."

"What was it like for you when she died?"

"I was pissed. I'm still pissed. Mourning the mother I had and the mother I never got was very hard. I'm still so mad at her.

"The last time I saw her alive was on Valentine's Day. Thank God she made an effort to see us on Valentine's Day that year. She drove to Ashlynn's dance school and met us out in the dark parking lot after ballet class was over. It was so cold, we could see our breath, and my mother was wrapped in her long white faux-fur coat. We hopped around in search of warmth and hugged and kissed a happy Valentine's Day to each other. She gave Ashlynn some candy. That was a Tuesday. Then, that Friday, she was dead."

I explained the events that led up to the discovery of my dead mother's body with clarity, without hesitation or emotion. I articulate with honest detail my thoughts and opinions, I had nothing left to lose. I wanted help so badly, it felt as if I was begging. And yet, I still wanted her to know that I was an intelligent woman, so I went straight to the point. The facts were all that mattered—another tight rubber band.

———

I roll up what I've removed of the rose-patterned green material and toss it into the wood stove. I watch the dusty fabric burn. I'm cremating this layer, like the red velour, sending it to its final resting place. I give my historically uptight self the same compassionate closure. I press the metal door of the stove closed. With the closure, I say, "I wasn't stupid. I was a result of my youth—lacking guidance, support, and belief in myself as a person."

I need to be compassionate with myself.

"That takes practice," I say to the loveseat.

There are so many details to any particular life. Every moment is impactful, and they compile over the years, creating a life. These are the standards that define our happiness. The infinity of early experiences is what I use as examples in my adult life.

No childhood moment was absent of torment—shadows like symptoms of the bigger, scarier, and unchanged horrors of my parents, their parents, and their grandparents. Genetic and hereditary, environmental and emotional, unbroken cycles cast shadows onto our souls and wreak havoc on our hearts.

We can hide our life's nightmares—bury them. At some point, if we stop resurrecting them, we will forget them. But who will they hurt along the way?

I told my therapist, "I learned from my devastating childhood history how to weed out unnecessary bullshit and get right to the point. All the polite, casual nuances of a happy life, happy workplace, and happy family were always missing. As an adult, I can barely tolerate small talk. Displays of interest about me and my life resonate with an insincerity I feel to my core.

"I absolutely hate when people ask me questions. I truly believe it's not for my benefit, but to satisfy their curiosity or create an opportunity to tell me something they want to talk about. Small talk with my husband is brutal too. It makes me want to get in my car and drive as far away as I can."

The therapist said, "I don't want to focus our sessions on

your husband, or your current state of mind. Not right now anyway. I want to peel back your layers."

Like the layers of this couch, I felt tattered and worn, decayed and torn. I opened up to my therapist, and I told her truths I'd never said aloud. My tale began to unfold, beginning with my mother's death.

"My mother would visit her father and my brother at least once a month. They live a few hours north of here, in Bar Harbor, where the family all comes from. 'If I didn't visit them, I'd never see them,' my mother would say.

"My brother, Casey, ended up back there after over a decade of moving around. Our mother moving us around, her many men, and her heartbreaks were bad for him. He never recovered. He became depressed, self-medicated with drugs, was in and out of rehab centers his entire life. He's now a forty-seven-year-old drug addict who lives according to his pain. Maybe I live according to my pain, too, just with a different expression of the same shit. Sometimes I feel like an addict, even though I don't use any substances. Does that make sense?"

"Yes. It makes sense because you grew up anticipating chaos. You were always expecting something, similar to the way an addict is always looking for something, and that doesn't just go away. You have to work and train your brain to believe that's not normal.

"Tell me about your mother's death. She lived in Portland when she died?"

"Yes. Why did my mother love this fucking city? It's cold, windy, and everyone acts as if you're a pain in the ass. There's nowhere to park, there's litter everywhere, people asking for your money, and just utter sadness everywhere you look." More anger and hate poured from my insides.

I understand now that the eruptions of anger and hate happening within me were all symptoms of my mental illness. Fear and pain were manifesting into expressions of animosity or rage, and I was overwhelmed with feelings of chaos. I excused all of these things away as survival mechanisms and coping skills.

"Except in the art district," I add. It's the only place in any city where happiness is believable. It looks like people there feel joy just from being themselves, looking like themselves, and practicing whatever mode of creative expression suits them. How do those people get that way? How were they raised? Where do they find that inner peace and confidence that I assume they must have?

"My mother's autopsy revealed that she had had a massive subarachnoid hemorrhaging stroke. The pathologist concluded that her stroke occurred because of her history of smoking one to two packs of cigarettes per day for over half of her life and frequent alcohol use.

"She lived her life for the party. The excitement that came from getting drunk and hooking up. She had many boyfriends. She was always with someone different, and they were always younger than her. Sometimes she'd get back together with someone who'd previously cheated on her.

Sometimes it was and ex-boyfriend of one of her sisters or friends. My mother began hanging out with and dating some of my acquaintances from school once they were old enough to go to bars. I'm sure most were one-night stands."

———

Remembering that I told my therapist about my mother sleeping with my classmates makes me tear up. The pang of fear and embarrassment settles in my throat. I turn away from the love seat and glance at the cobwebs tracing the basement ceiling. Tears fill my eyes and drain at the corners. I wipe at them with my wrist, avoiding my dirtied and blood-ied knuckles. I squeeze my fingers into the crevice between the backrest and the seat cushion. I feel some granules of dirt with my fingertips and then a chain. I pull out a thin silver chain that a previous owner had lost. At its end dangles a tiny heart pendant. "Huh."

———

"In my mother's eyes, I was always her best friend," I said to my therapist. "She told me all of her secrets and tragedies. She literally told me what she did during sex; and not only that, but she shared every detail of numerous incidents that should never be discussed with or heard by any human being besides a trained professional. To hear such secrets about my mom, dad, aunt, uncle, grandparents—well, it meant I would never be able to live a normal life.

"When I was eighteen years old, after I finished high

school, my mother encouraged me to drink alcohol with her and brought me to bars and clubs. My mother loved that we could party together; she would smoke cigarettes, I could drink, and she would get a guy. Many nights out ended with my mother leaving with random guy my age.

"My mother went through a stage of only dating black men. They were always younger than her, and sometimes younger than me. The color of a person's skin doesn't matter. What mattered to me was that it seemed to matter to her. 'I can't do what people expect me to do,' she would say. 'I want to surprise people.' I'm ashamed to say that dating men with a particular skin color became her primary objective for about fifteen years of her dating life—all for the sake of shock value. But for who? My dad? Her dad? Likely both.

"By the time I was twenty-five years old, I'd had enough and told her that I didn't want to party with her anymore. It was my attempt at setting a boundary.

"I tried to explain how it hurt me to do these things with her and that I was worried she had a drinking problem. She made me suffer for speaking up, badgering me about it throughout the rest of her life. I wish I had never said a word. I couldn't have a relationship with her if my needs dictated it. She was so terrible to me in every encounter we had after that one conversation.

"'I'll never be the mother you want me to be. You want me to just sit at home and make cookies and waste my life,' she'd say, and I'd reply, 'Sorry, I'm a life-waister, Mom.' Then she'd say, 'I would never judge you that way,' or, 'Stop acting like such a bitch and do something for someone else for once.' She accused me of kicking her to the curb because I didn't want to drink with her anymore.

"When she died, I was forced to say goodbye to the woman I wanted her to be—her abrupt and unexpected death made me realize I would never have the mother I needed and longed for. I had to say goodbye to the hope of finding that mother inside of her somehow. And goodbye to the woman she was who I loved and would miss desperately. The woman that had spent most of her time on earth, from age fifteen to fifty-seven, effectively fucking up my brother and me."

After this first hour with my therapist, I was exhausted. I spoke of these experiences with my mother as if they were no big deal. I explained them as if these tragedies were ordinary. I held onto the belief that I needed to act strong, intelligent, and ensure her that I could weather these storms. What she heard in this first session was only the beginning. I had so much more to tell.

Chapter Fourteen

Intricate Coils of Spring-Work

Removing the green fabric was the easiest of all. The nails holding it on had rusted enough so that pulling them from the wood was easy. The cloth was in relatively good condition, considering how old it must have been. The cuts—I decided they were knife strokes—that had ripped the beautiful red velour didn't injure this layer at all.

I find a penny from 1906 between the backrest and seat cushion. I see more gravel and multiple toothpicks. I employ the Shop-Vac and suck out anything left inside the couch's crevices.

Pulling off this layer of textile exposes me to the bones of the furniture. Decades of dirt empties onto the floor and floats through the air. Dust-filled stuffing adheres to the fabric. I roll up each piece and toss it into the roaring wood stove. The green of the material reminds me of our trailer in Hulls Cove.

I become fixated with watching it burn. I think about how poor we were; and I remember the dark green stripe painted all the way around and about halfway up the otherwise all-white trailer. I remember how my mother's vehicles were garbage, and our refrigerator only ever contained lettuce or apples. The canned peaches or fruit cocktail from The Bargain Barn often ended up with a giant black bug of some kind at the bottom of the can. The bug's presence never deterred us from eating it, though. Food was scarce and precious.

"I found another cricket in the peaches," I would announce and continue eating.

I think about when she only had a motorcycle to get us around. She would drive us to school one at a time. And summers were spent alone with my brother in the trailer while our mother worked.

My time with my therapist brought clarity to so many moments. Each session was an hour of me answering one question at a time. My answers were direct but lengthy.

———

"Tell me about where you lived when you were growing up," she asked.

"Mom moved us in and out of her parents' house. It depended on if she was getting along with my father or if she wasn't dating someone else. We lived in three different places on one street. I can count six homes in Bar Harbor alone. In kindergarten, we moved to Waterville for a short time. My mother's older brother, Forrest, lived there. I was in kindergarten, so my mom was nineteen or twenty.

"Eventually, we moved back to Bar Harbor. My mother bought a trailer—a real home. I wondered if this would be the beginning of having the mother and father I needed and the home I craved. Maybe it would happen. We were buying a trailer. This type of purchase proved commitment to the family, I thought. I had hope then.

"What I mostly remember of my life at that trailer was losing that hope. A vast feeling of loss and heartache sums up our time there. All of those dreams shattered before they had a chance. I have many memories of my mother and father arguing so loud that it hurt my ears, and so often, they convinced me that this was how life would always be. It was a nonstop battle between them. Dad would chase my mother through the house, her feet pounding from room to room. I hated it so much I wished they would break up for good.

"Listening to my parents fight over and over again was like being in the middle of a violent war that never ends. The sounds tore at my insides cramping my soul into an imploded void. I bottled the pain up inside of me. I absorbed their arguments, and it felt like burning sharp-edged coals. Once absorbed, they didn't dissipate. They've remained inside of me forever. I can still feel them now, to this day. I'm fucking forty-three years old, and I can still feel the pain."

I point one finger into the air, "One memory and emotion stands out to me as the utterly worst loss I have ever felt. Maybe it was because I was old enough to comprehend it, or perhaps it was so vivid because I erroneously assumed it was the last chance we had. It hurt bad; it hurt like hell. I would describe the pain as worse than giving birth and worse than putting a knife into your chest. It's when my mom forced my father to leave.

"He had lived with us for an unusually long period. Maybe a few months? Long enough that he took care of my brother and me at night when our mother was at work. He let us take turns staying up late one night a week each. And we got to pick the television show we watched with him. I picked *Mork and Mindy* when it was my turn.

"I don't know what happened. I assume my dad was unfaithful. He always was.

"I wanted him to stay. I wanted to hold onto him and never let him go. I cried. I begged. 'No, Daddy, don't go.' The thought of him leaving crushed me. My chest felt heavier than my small frame could carry. I followed him to the door. Tears soaked my face so much I could barely see. He didn't say goodbye. He didn't hug me. He didn't tell me it would be okay. My mother hollered curse words, and said, 'Get the fuck out of here, Tarzan.'

"I could see the pain in his face. I could see that he may have been hurting as much as I did, and that made it worse. He moved quickly, with rigid limbs. And I saw more sadness in his features than I had ever seen. At that moment, I saw through his tough exterior and beyond the legend of Tarzan. I saw a man who needed love. And perhaps his expression of this need is through the man he is: The life of the party. The tough guy and bad boy. The beyond brave and crazy heartthrob who smokes cigarettes while pumping gas into his Harley Davidson. The name and reputation everyone in town knows—Tarzan.

"My chest heaved, and I didn't think I would survive the

moment. I was so scared that I wanted to scream. I needed to allow my feelings to erupt and boil within me. But I held it in. I knew my scream would never be louder than theirs. In their fights, no one ever won; I certainly wouldn't. No one would hear my scream, not for what it truly meant. I would be scolded and shamed, and they would not see me. They would look through me like a piece of glass, and I would shatter.

"And the shattering would remain internal, as always. The shattering of my hope, my heart, and my soul would ravage me with internal injury. And I wouldn't show it. Perhaps my eyes would drop to the floor. Maybe my shoulders would hunch forward, or I would put my hand to my gut. But they would never see or know the pain in me.

"Why could we not have peace? Love?

"A family that loved me is all I wanted. I wanted them to love me. I wanted them to acknowledge me. But instead, my parents ignored me and lived for themselves. I was so far from the center of their attention that I didn't exist.

"The pain in my chest was so big I couldn't swallow it this time. And yet, I was alone. I was invisible. My mother ignored my sadness and wept for her own. He walked out, without hesitation, turning his back to me. He didn't touch me, look at me, or even hear me. I retreated to my tiny bedroom. The same bedroom where I once walked in on two naked people, my parents' friends, having sex in my bed. They didn't stop when walked in. I closed the door and waited until they finished. 'Jesus, Tina, don't worry, I'll wash the damn sheets,' my mother said when I told her.

"It wasn't the sheets that upset me. At the time, I had no idea why I was upset, but I felt so sad and heavy. I couldn't stop crying. From my blank, emotionless face, tears leaked uncontrollably from my eyes. My mouth went limp and drool streamed to my shirt, and I kept it all to myself. I felt sick and alone, and a boulder lodged in my throat.

"Still, that same bed was my only place to go to find comfort after my dad left. I climbed under the protection of my under-washed blankets in a bed smaller than a twin. I sat in a corner alone and sobbed. I hugged myself and closed my eyes tight.

"Within the blackness of my closed eyes, I saw floating dots of all colors—an apparition of twirling lights. They would come to me in times of intense sadness. I called them my friends. They swirled and shined, my stars accompanying me in my grief. There were times they didn't come, and I wished for them desperately. In those moments of aloneness, when I couldn't even count on the colorful stars I conjured in my mind; I think I accepted that I couldn't count on anything.

————

I stop pulling at the tacks holding the green fabric in place. I close my watering eyes to behold the blackness behind my eyelids. I try to call upon my friends. The floating dots I used to see as a child. My eyes remain closed. I wait for them and smile at myself. They do not come. I cannot conjure them because I'm okay now. I open my eyes and stand up to stretch. A head rush causes me to clutch the armrest. Once it passes, I bend down and return to the repetitive act of pulling nails and exploring my memories of sadder times as I explained them to my therapist.

―――――

"We called the trailer home for a few years. So many moments of horror passed. I can remember one moment of physical affection from my father. He returned in the middle of the night, unannounced, and woke me. He turned on my bedroom light and pulled me from the warmth of my covers and into his lap. He kissed my face and rocked me in his arms. I could smell his breath. I can still smell that moment. He was drunk. I felt his love. I knew he wished our lives were different. But he didn't know how.

"My mother called him George that night. He was my father at that moment. He wasn't Tarzan, my mother's lover, but my father, George.

"'George, leave her alone. She was sleeping.'

"'I just want to hug my baby girl.' He said as he squeezed me. It felt good and scary all at the same time. He kissed my cheeks with a slobbering mouth. Again, I smelled his breath.

"'I don't see you for days, and you come here in the middle of the night and wake us all up? Put her back to bed, George.'

"He loved me, but he didn't know how to show it. Intoxicated love was enough for me. I will never forget that moment. I realize now that he likely forgot within the hour that it had happened at all. For me, it was a lifetime of love in an act that took him all of two minutes to perform.

"The summer before sixth grade, my mother made another big move—to Portland. According to my mother, we had to move to get away from my father's reputation.

"She did it for our sake." My tone was sarcastic.

———

Clutching the dusty stuffing that had been housed within the couch for decades, I pull it from the elaborate spring system below. I can feel granules of dirt and coarse horsehair between my fingers. I toss it into the wood stove and it erupts into hot flames. Heat scorches the skin on my fingers as I continue to throw handfuls of the aged stuffing into the fire.

———

I remember the gray-and-black striped carpet that separated my therapist's chair from where I sat. I detest the memory of my father leaving. Another scar unchanged with time. The physical impact of trauma from my youth returns with each revisit. I can feel it as I felt it at the moment.

"I cannot recall the pain of childbirth like this. My body ripped to allow the passage of my baby. A pain I can sort of recall and would endure again without question. But I can clearly remember the pain of my childhood traumas, and I would not choose to go through them again. The pain I felt the day my mother kicked my father out of the trailer is as present now as it was the day it happened." My therapist wrote something on her pad.

The hour had passed. My therapist tilted her head toward the clock. I stopped talking and pulled in a long breath. I held it in and then let it out very slow.

"I want to give you a relaxation exercise, Tina. I want you to use visualization during moments of stress. It's simple but effective. I want you to pick an object, like a school bus or a taxi, and visualize it. I hope that you will redirect your brain and stop these processes of stress. Does that sound like something you can do?"

"Yes."

"Also, I don't want you to engage in intimacy until you want intimacy. Can you do that?"

"Yes."

Chapter Fifteen

Ebony Stain

As I vacuum the last of the horsehair and dirt from the floor under the love seat, I recall facing my therapist for my second appointment.

Her couch leaned against the inside wall of her small office, which overlooked the city and Portland harbor. The sofa's thick textured fabric with obviously identifiable fibers reminded me of hay. She had few pictures on the walls. The one above the couch was large and appeared to be swirls of unrecognizable shapes in blue hues. The other was an enlarged photo of the ocean.

She sat in her usual chair in front of the windows, across from me and to my left. "I like having something for my patients to look at besides me, so I offer the outside," she said. I didn't respond.

The perfume I wore back then was always too strong. Sometimes it made me uncomfortable, but I couldn't put on less. I tried so hard but always added one too many squirts. I hoped the aroma boasted confidence at first scent but revealed a sweet, sultry undertone. Sort of a surprise lingering after your nose adjusts. More ridiculous intentions to appear confident and sexy.

She waited for me to speak. I felt differently than I did during our first meeting. I felt more vulnerable. I allowed myself to be soft and weak, as if my rubber bands had loosened. I didn't make as much eye contact, my face felt hot, and my neck itched with hives. I was overwhelmed with a sadness that sat heavy in my stomach.

I had so much more that needed to be said. I had so much pain and heartache, I could feel it in my face. Anguish reddened my cheeks. I carried the kind of grief that changes your face when it teeters at the edge of your psyche—I know it changed mine. I looked like a near relative with similar features but not that same woman she met the week before. I was suffering from pain and anger, and I wanted to let it all go.

I didn't bring any of the false attempts to appear more assertive than I was. I didn't care if my therapist judged me. I didn't have the energy to maintain any appearance of having a high IQ or the ability to survive hard things. This undoing rendered me speechless.

My therapist began talking since I couldn't. "How did the visualization exercise go?"

"I don't think it went well."

"How come?"

"I imagined a school bus and a taxi, and eventually, they ended up smashing into each other."

She covered her smile with her hand. "I hoped you would come up with your own object to visualize. Something that brings you happiness without any guilt. Try it again, but think of something you feel zen and tranquil about next time."

"Okay," I said.

"Tina, I help my patients based on science and intuition. The science I studied to obtain my degrees, but I'm also a human being. I can see you're hurting. I have a way of seeing inside my patients simply by paying attention. I can read body language, eye contact, the quiver of tiny muscles in faces or propensities for fidgeting or stillness, breathing rate, flushing, sincerity, or evasiveness.

"I can see inside of you, Tina, right now. It's as if you're sending me an urgent and intense telepathic message. If you could say it out loud, it might be something like: 'I need help. My sadness is more profound than I know how to handle, and the mere thought of not being able to control something will kill me with its chaos. Please help me find peace.'"

I took a long, slow, deep breath, looked her straight in the eyes, and teared up. I was relieved. She could see me. She got it, and she understood me. I was not a transparent piece of glass she looked through. I was not invisible. I felt as if I could step out of at least one rubber band and leave it on her floor that day. My throat relaxed for a moment and then tightened again. My throat filled with relief, and with sadness that it had taken this long to be validated.

I began to speak. I was very animated with my hands, and I struggled to get the words out. I held back tears and my sorrow as best I could. I could hear the tightness in my throat coming through as I voiced my feelings. The tightness expanded into my chest and caused pain in my neck. My face was flushed red, and I trembled as if shivering.

"My daughter is thirteen years old, and I am overwhelmed with trying to protect her from everything. I don't want her to know that I'm unhappy or angry. I don't want her to think that all men are pigs. I don't want her to know about anything I have ever done or that my parents did that causes me to feel shame. I can't be there when her sociopathic, narcissistic father fucks with her brain. I can't be there when he hurts her and makes her cry. When he makes her feel like she's a piece of shit. I want to stop allowing him to make me feel like I'm a piece of shit.

"When I left him, we had to share custody. I know that when I had to leave her with her father, she didn't understand where Mommy went. All of a sudden, I went from being her primary caregiver to seeing her every other week. She was only two years old, and I was gone half the time. I couldn't be there to protect her, hold her, and help her. I am so sorry about that, and I will never forgive myself for not being there when she needed me. But I had to leave her father. He'd convinced me that everything I did was wrong in some way. I believed that I was terrible, untrustworthy, insignificant, and an incapable mother. I had lost myself.

"Only after she was born did I realize just how lost I was. With her birth, I realized that I needed to protect her from my relationship with her father; I couldn't let her experience the evil between us, the evil in him. All I knew how to do was live my life for him, and she needed to see me live my life for her and me. Deep down I knew anytime our daughter spent with him would harm her. I had no way of explaining it and no-one else saw him for his true self. He had never been her caretaker. She needed to be with me primarily, but he wouldn't let me have primary custody, and everyone believed everything horrible he said about me.

"Hell, I believed him.

"Leaving him was one of the hardest things I have ever done, and it was because he tormented me and broke me down. He's punished me every day since I left him. He is so mentally ill and cunning that the stress and shame I felt for leaving made me physically ill. I got a sinus infection that needed two rounds of antibiotics. I developed an intestinal infection that felt like a monster living inside of my body."

"C diff?" asked my therapist.

"Yes. It was the sickest I have ever been. I dropped twenty pounds that I didn't have to lose. I'm sure I could have died if I didn't receive treatment in time. I know the stress of dealing with his constant attacks and threats had something to do with how sick I became.

"And I believe he'll never stop. Every day he pushes me deeper into believing I'm not worthy of our daughter or of being happy. I cannot ward off the injury of his words and the fear he instills in me. Leaving your abuser is so scary that it feels impossible." Then I whispered, "But, I did it." The only good thing I had to say about myself.

"I desperately want my daughter to be happy. She is perfect. She is the most precious thing to me in this world. I want her to be satisfied with who she is and what she has to offer, as she is, without any change. I want her to feel free to be herself, passionate about what makes her happy, and not get hurt. I want her to feel the internal quiet that comes with the ability to trust. While I want this for her, I can't do it for myself.

"I don't want to fake happiness anymore. I want to love my husband, and I want her to experience a healthy relationship between him and me. But my relationship is not healthy; I wouldn't know a healthy relationship if it hit me in the face.

"And I want to know that I'm doing it right—being a mother. Honestly, I have never believed that I am. Her father makes sure to point out all of my mistakes and inadequacies. I have no idea how to be firm when I need to be. Or even if I need to be. I try, but I'm insecure about every decision I make as a parent. There are so many things I need to teach her that I have no idea how to do myself.

"My childhood trauma has become part of the building blocks of who I am. Instead of strong solid blocks, mine are weak, uneven, and shaky. My building blocks have been tormented to the point that there is a constant disturbance, which ruins any chance of me building a productive, happy life upon them. My foundation was weak. But all I show the world is that I'm strong. I know I'm not authentic to anyone, including my daughter, and I have no idea how to be. Or to be okay with it either way."

My therapist gave me a moment of silence. I stared at my hands in my lap. They were heavy from holding all of my rubber bands across my thighs. Tears leaked down to my quivering chin. My chest heaved, and I tried to compose myself.

"What kind of love would you like to feel right now with your husband?"

"The only true love I am capable of is the love I feel for my daughter. There is no room for any other love. I love her beyond words, and I would give my life for her. There is no one else in this world I could feel that way about."

"Do you believe that there are other kinds of love beyond the kind you feel for your daughter?"

"I guess there must be. But if I can give anyone else love, shouldn't it be myself? I don't have any for myself. I think that causes me to have no patience or tolerance for anyone else who demands my love. Pets, my husband, relatives, friends. Well, I go through stages—right now, I feel no love for anyone else besides Ashlynn. Sometimes, rarely, I soften enough to feel it for others. Hell, I don't know what I feel."

I mentioned my daughter's name. It surprised me when I said it, and I wished I could take it back. I was so protective that my instinct was to keep Ashlynn's name out of this room so I could shield her from the disclosure of evil things. Saying her name brought her here, and I didn't want that. I shook my head.

"Can we talk about your daughter's dad?"

"Yes."

"Were you married?"

"Yes. I met Lance when I was twenty-three. I had just graduated from college and was in need of some boundaries.

He had no problem providing them. Let me just say that I lived my entire life before him with constant trauma; then, I dove headfirst into more when I met him.

"I felt a love and adoration for him that I had never experienced before. It all started because I found him so incredibly handsome. He was a bodybuilder; well, a powerlifter. The first time I saw him, I thought he was a giant, and I loved that. Powerful in body and mind. I will honestly say his control is precisely what I needed in my early twenties.

"I needed to be wrapped up tight. I required that metaphorical weighted blanket that I was still searching for.

"He told me when to kiss him and how to kiss him. He insisted that I must kiss him every time I said hello or goodbye. Obeying his commands was the proper way to be a girlfriend. 'Don't you ever get out of this truck again without giving me a kiss first.' He ordered me to give him attention and insisted that he should be the center of my world and that no one else mattered. He was jealous and controlling. It made me feel loved.

"I fed on the pain of our relationship. I had learned that pain was part of a relationship between a man and a woman. I had become accustomed to measuring love by the existence of pain.

"I wanted to make him feel secure and confident. I tried to make his life easier, and I wanted to have a family like the one I'd never had growing up—one with a wife, a husband, children that are cherished, a dog, a house, trust, and love. We got married when I was twenty-five.

"He was volatile and very emotionally abusive. I could

not trust him with anything in confidence. He would use everything I told him against me. He would point out my imperfections, emotional shortcomings, and details about my family that would make me eventually push them away. I believed him most of the time. I thought that I was fucked up and no one else would ever love me. No one had ever seen me or acknowledged me the way he did, so his assessment of my imperfections must have been accurate. Right?

"I was a bad wife, and I needed to be more attentive. Or I thought I needed to ignore everyone else in a room to assure him I was in love with him and that I was not checking out other men.

"We had so many fights in public, so many times he treated me like a piece of trash, or he would initiate an explosive argument and leave me wherever we were without caring about how I'd get home. I had learned from my mother's life that relationships were painful, and this physically beautiful man was better than me, so I needed to make it work.

"Shortly after we were married, my niece, Carley, was born. Casey and his very young girlfriend, Amy, had a baby girl. I fell in love with her, and I loved how that felt. It was unlike anything I had experienced. I ached to have a baby of my own after falling in love with her.

"My first pregnancy ended in miscarriage. I was heartbroken and inconsolable. I blamed myself, of course. I wasn't a good enough woman to be a mother. I didn't even have my own boobs. Finally, a year later, my heartache ended when we conceived our daughter.

"I remember asking myself how this was going to be possible? How could I grow a baby and give birth? It seemed unlikely and that I was not worthy of such a miracle. But to my surprise, she thrived. I was so happy. I was actually becoming a mother. Me—this insignificant person who was born to a world of unhappy people where I didn't make a difference in anyone's life, except my husband's and now, soon, my baby's.

"However, when she was born, I was immediately scared shitless, and felt insecure. I love her so much that, even now, I fear that I'm not a good enough mother to her. But back then, it was worse. We brought her home, and I felt panic. I was not good enough for this perfect angel.

"In tears, I went to Lance and told him I was scared and didn't know what to do or how to take care of her. He used that against me from that day forward. At the very moment I needed compassion, Lance reminded me what a weak and imperfect person I was. Luckily, I don't deal well with imperfection, so I vowed to become the perfect mother. I promised that she would have the ideal childhood, she would grow up with way more than I ever had, and she would be loved and happy.

"I read parenting books, and I emulated Marcy, one of my best friends from college. Everything she did, I did.

"And now, after thirteen years, I am still convinced that I can't do it. Her childhood was not perfect and was full of fear for her. And I'm still failing, and I feel like I'm going to explode."

"Tina, there is no such thing as perfect. Life is a compilation of lessons and growth."

I know, I said to myself. Aloud, I answered, "Accepting that perfection isn't possible is imperfect and proof of my imperfection."

"Tina, you mentioned trust. Tell me about trust in your life," said my therapist.

I took a deep breath and crossed my arms in my lap, cradling my elbows in my hands. I pressed my boney knees together, and I spread my feet apart with my heels pointed out while my toes pointed in. I felt like a little girl all dressed up in her mother's clothes. My black tuxedo-style jacket, black pencil skirt, black hose, and high-heeled booties were sharp as a tack. My hair, pulled to a low side bun, was rigid with hairspray to ensure not one single strand was out of place. My faux diamond earrings sparkled, and the matching faux diamond-with-pearl necklace fell just above the rise of my chest, threatening to scrape the thin skin on my protruding collarbone.

I slumped. My shoulders rolled forward. Today, I had surrendered my usual rigid, uptight demeanor, but I was still dressed the part.

"I have been told by my mother and shown by my father since the day I was born that NO man is trustworthy. Like so many men out there, my father had every reason to remain faithful and everything to lose but still decided to be unfaithful. That is why I have lost my faith—or why I never had any. There is nothing more precious to a man than sex."

"Someday, you will see that that is not true," said my therapist.

"I saw my father very rarely as a child or as a teenager or as an adult. I have never really spent much time with him. I spent occasional weekends with him after he got sober and some holidays. I loved him. The time I got to spend with him was precious to me. He would often leave while I was there. While my brother and I were there. 'I have to go, Tina. I just have to go. Everyone is out on their motorcycles, and they want me to come. I can't say no.'

"There were many times I'd babysit Casey and the kids of whoever he was out with for the night when I was way too young to babysit, and I needed a sitter myself. Once, I was caring for a baby, but I had no idea how to feed a baby or change a diaper. I couldn't even lift him. He was half my size.

"Oh, and it appears I carried on the family trait of sharing men. I'm not proud to say that I dated a guy my aunt, Berta, had sort of dated briefly. She and I were sort of close growing up. After I became a teenager, she became unfriendly, rude and mean to me. Maybe that is why I dated him? To get her back. We didn't speak for years. I just thought that it was what family does to each other. I felt terrible doing it, but I still did it, and now I put myself right down there at the same shitty level with my mother who did it to Berta and my aunt and grandmother who had sex with my dad.

"Pain equals love. I have never known painless love.

"Like I should love my grandfather even though he is a

mean, selfish asshole who never protected his three daughters and two sons from his bullshit temper or pedophile friends.

"I hate that man. He has no love for me. Why should I love him despite all of this? Because he was an orphan and multiple families used him for child labor? Because he never had a real family? Because he never had shoes, money, food, or clothes growing up?"

"You are angry at your grandfather."

"I guess. I think I'm angry because no one else complains about his bullshit. But it's not just my grandfather. I'm pissed at a lot of people—my mom, my dad, my brother, myself, my husband."

———

The solid wood legs of the antique couch are light brown. All past applications of protective polyurethane have worn off. I find a piece of fine sandpaper, cup it in my palm, and press it to the aged wood. I begin a rhythm of small circles. I don't particularly enjoy sanding, but my brother, the genius painter, insists on it. I begin, attempting not to miss an inch, but I'm soon irritated and focus on only the prominent areas. Wood dust settles into the carved design, and I blow it out with my breath.

Once I have sanded the legs, the wooden rise of the arms, and the curved edge over the back, I find a clean paintbrush to sweep out the dust from the hand-carved designs and onto the floor. The nearby Shop-Vac assists me further with removing most of the particles. I complete preparing the wood for staining with a wet cloth. I pass it along all of the wooden surfaces, wiping away anything I missed.

I locate the can of stain that I purchased for this project. It's one of my favorite wood stain colors: ebony. It's such a dark brown that it can sometimes appear black.

I remember when, after a few years of therapy, my therapist and I directed our time and attention to Ashlynn's biological father:

———

"What about Ashlynn's father," asked my therapist.

"It's only now that I can explain what life and divorce were like with Ashlynn's father. I have always considered myself a decently intelligent woman. Yet, I could not define him. His behavior was beyond words for me at the time. I was a wounded shell that the world perceived as the wrongdoer in my relationship with him. The Guardian ad Litem sided with him, and the courts saw no reason why Ashlynn shouldn't be with him half the time. My best friend disowned me for leaving him. What an ass I must have been.

"There is something about a narcissistic sociopath that allows them to exist under everyone else's radar. Ashlynn once called it his superpower. And I agree. Every word he speaks, every action, intention, and outcome of a situation has been a thoughtfully constructed orchestration by a cunning compulsion to overpower—the toxic desire to render the kindest, most giving human being guilt-ridden and confused. And the entire time, no one can put their finger on how he does it.

"Consider the word narcissistic: its curvaceous pronunciation–the incline of *narc*, and the river of *issistic*. How can such a poetic expression describe the havoc inflicted on your psyche by a person labeled as such?

"The dictionary definition is much too compressed. It reads something like: a narcissist seeks admiration for their physical and mental attributes. Isn't that a normal human desire? What's missing from the dictionary are the multi-leveled intensities with which narcissism displays itself. To be exact, how is the admiration sought? Is it a harmless acquisition? Or is it at the expense of another person's soul?

"Subtle tricks of the mind, a posture, a look, a word—all camouflaged by deception and secret code.

"A narcissist's most remarkable ability is brilliant manipulation executed in invisible terms; seamlessly captivating the unaware with his charms. At first, you're unaware of his deadly sting, allowing him to seduce you easily into his web. His superpower unfolds and he can convince you of anything without a conscious plot to do so. No planning, rehearsing, or premeditation needed; instead, it comes naturally to him. Injurious, verbal sticks-and-stones that shatter your backbone to reinforce his.

"Somehow, he knew me. And he knew he would beat me at his game. I thought I knew suffering before him. After I met him, I discovered a new kind of suffering. I questioned my intentions, beliefs, and abilities while I embarked on a desperate quest to obtain whatever remedy he required to believe in my adoration and commitment. His happiness and satisfaction became my only priority.

"His wants and happiness now superseded my own. I was only okay if he was. I lost what little voice I had. I was flawed, even worse than I had imagined, and he was near perfection. Every decision I made was wrong, and I was—am—ashamed. I was embarrassed because I should have known better. I shouldered his blame and covered for his lousy behavior. I wanted to help him—after all, he needed me. My guess, it was because I could see his weaknesses, and I longed for his love, so I continued to chase what he dangled just out of my reach.

"I continued until I lost everything. Lance was counting on it. His goal was for me to lose my sanity, lose my money getting him out of debt, lose my determination, friends, family, and happiness. Shame blinded my vision of the truth of him.

"How did this happen?" I asked my therapist. She took a breath and opened her mouth to answer, but I interrupted.

"All of the red flags from that first day, the first month, then the first five years of our relationship now seem so obvious."

"Can you give me some examples?"

"In 1993, the sight of him took my breath away. He towered over every other muscle-bound powerlifter inside Union Station Gym. He carried a leather weightlifting belt as large as my entire torso. His legs bulged like a Greek god's, and I melted into his green eyes.

"One of his friends asked me out on a date for him. I said yes. How could such a massive and beautiful older man be so shy? Especially about asking me out? Me: a tall skinny girl with no figure and no good sense. I came from a low-income family and a small town and was in my last year of college. Me?

"On our first date, I drove to his apartment, arrived five minutes late, and before I could close the door to my car, he was out of the house and headed toward me with quick wide steps. His first words that day were, 'You're late.' He continued past me, his chest pressed forward and his arms pulled out from his hips wider than necessary. His black leather jacket was unzipped, and his tight black jeans stretched around his wide legs. He motioned for me to get into his truck with a smile. I was a little startled by his comment, but not sure if it was just a joke. I swallowed my tentativeness and got in his truck.

"He was interested in me. Me, in my entirety, and promised to give me everything I never had but unquestionably deserved from my thoughtless family. Finally, a man who would put me first, I thought. His magic had begun, and I was under his spell.

"I shrugged off his violent outrages and pub brawls with strangers as admissions of insecurity, along with his demands that I not walk ahead of him, ever, and that I must hold his arm and talk to him, and only him, when we were in public, otherwise people would think I didn't care about him. 'Is that how a wife acts?' and 'You better act like you love me,' were things he whispered into my ears in public. Lance never whispered sweet nothings of love or kindness. Instead, his voice was so firm my eardrums ached and felt as if they could bleed from the sheer volume of his ruthless demands for me to comply with his needs.

"I remember his lies to trick me into admitting nonexistent guilt and his jealousy over past relationships, family, and friends that somehow became justified. He would always use my secrets against me. I shrugged it all off. I'd seen my mother put up with shit like this, and I believed pain proved commitment. I thought that our love was worth the struggle and the difficulty.

"I now know that I could take it because, as weak as I was, I was stronger than him. I would prove my commitment and my love in light of the difficulty by not only putting up with his bullshit but also excusing it.

"Not one day passed without incident. Not one week passed without me crying until my eyes were emptied of all of their tears. But I was determined that my dreams of having a stable family and children would not elude me. I would make sure it happened, and this relationship was not going to fail. I told myself that I could fix this.

"And as our life progressed, we had a baby girl. The day she was born was the first day of my life that I felt true love. The mother inside me woke up. I became enlightened with a sense of purpose, and it wasn't to serve a man who held bitterness and distrust in his heart toward his child and me.

"In 2003, though I was weak and my courage was tender, I left him. My family helped me move my belongings, but I lacked their full support. No one trusted me. No one told me not to take his shit. No one said I was right and he was wrong. No one told me to call the police if I needed to. Instead, everyone questioned my motives. They didn't see the truth of him, or they didn't believe in me—probably both. It was the hardest thing I have ever done; the second was when I supported our daughter leaving him in 2015.

"Ashlynn struggled to grow up with him." I take a deep breath and close my eyes. "I could have helped her better. I didn't explain the truth about him to her. I was so focused on not badmouthing her father the way my mother did mine that I kept my mouth shut about him—because of this, Ashlynn assumed his behavior as her fault. She took all of his criticisms and inconsistencies as a display of her shortcomings.

"I wasn't seeing her. I'm ashamed to say it, but I had hoped Lance would treat her differently than he treated me. By not validating everything she experienced and making it real, I wasn't seeing her. Just like my parents never saw me." I cried into my palms.

"She wasn't allowed to talk about me, show that she loved or missed me. Lance was very jealous of her life with me, so she couldn't talk about it unless it was something negative. He groomed her to distrust Billy. Lance punished her with silence and threats of leaving her if she wanted to spend extra time with me. He forced her to show him a disgusting level of affection, regardless of whether she wanted to or not. He left her alone to get herself ready for middle school in the mornings and wouldn't allow me to intervene. She was scared to be alone on these mornings but even more scared to death of him.

"At a very young age, Ashlynn began hitting herself in the face. She started having panic attacks and would cry herself into a comatose state. Ashlynn became suicidal; she cut her arms and fantasized about running away. She thought she was crazy. Ashlynn started seeing her counselor in eighth grade and continued until she went to college.

"When she was almost thirteen, it dawned on me that she needed to understand who he was. While not saying her father was a screwed-up person, I began identifying his behaviors aloud to her. I began telling her when he made me angry or when my opinions differed from his.

"We made up the dad dance. It was a rapid-fire foot stomping while shaking our fists at the ground and screaming our faces into crushed expressions. When we were furious with him, or when we felt so insignificant that we wanted to wither and die, or when we knew we couldn't change his bitter perspective, we did the dad dance.

"These changes from me were what she needed. And when she decided she didn't want to see her dad anymore, I fought like hell for her. I chose to risk jail time over allowing him to inflict any more pain on her.

"In not being honest with her about him, I recognized the moments from my high school years with my mother and my suicidal boyfriend from Missouri. Seeing the truth of her father was the only hope she had of living. And once I realized my error, I became her warrior against him."

"You should be very proud of that, Tina," my therapist said. I smiled and looked at my hands.

"Ashlynn and I have been through the same war with Lance. His brutality has scarred us both. He blames us for all of his actions, and the pressure of his blame was so heavy we almost drowned in shame. How could we leave such a wonderful, irreplaceable man? He said no one would ever love us like he did.

"Thank God."

————

I dip a two-inch-wide foam brush into the dark stain and spread the liquid across the dull, lifeless dry wood. The ebony stain covers the worn legs with hydration and shine. Again, I withdraw color from the can and paint. It absorbs into the sturdy shape of the wood. With it, I release the darkness of narcissistic injury and allow this antique couch to hold onto it for me. My mother's grief and her life of pain, along with mine, are now trapped in this artifact. I will forever appreciate the love I have for this piece, and in my labor comes the newness of hope. The hope obtained from lessons learned. And from the surrender of regret and fear.

I am stronger than him. Ashlynn is stronger than him.

And I believe we have always known that. If not, why would we have adapted our behavior to try to make him happy? Why would we have tried so hard to prove our loyalty? Why would we have shouldered blame that was not ours? Because we knew he was weak. Now I understand that his anger comes from weakness, his volatility comes from insecurity, and his abusive behavior comes from fear and shame. He promised to be the tender man we both needed until he didn't get his way. And because of that, he spent every waking hour over the course of sixteen years crushing and condemning me with his brutality.

I went from the extreme of no one seeing me as a child to the confines of one of the evilest men I could have found.

The pungent smell of wood stain clears my nose. Like how rubbing alcohol cleans, the astringent smell of paint purifies these moments from me and cures me of an illness. Until now, I have had a life so traumatic that it's only fair I accept the post-traumatic stress as part of my recovery. It, too, has passed. I have encouraged its healing by providing a forever home for new memories among aged pieces of furniture. It's time for me to pick up the shattered pieces of my heart and soul and learn how to protect and care for myself.

I have become a collector and rehabilitator of material objects that have been given up on, used, abused, neglected, and forgotten. We will share a happy home, and each collected piece will be a loving family member for the others.

Chapter Sixteen

A Royal Tapestry

The ebony stain requires twenty-four hours to set, and then the layer of polyurethane takes a solid forty-eight hours to dry. Meanwhile, I shop for new fabric at Joann's.

Billy dropped me off before heading to his favorite project supply store: Home Depot. I consider Joann Fabrics and Home Depot to be equivalent destinations for very different project doers. Both open early, both are the busiest stores on the weekends, and most customers carry measuring tape.

I scan the fabrics the same way I review items in antique stores. I see past the colors and textures that don't suit me. I touch the ones that appear soft and smile at the ones that glitter in the fluorescent lights. When I feel an attraction to a color or design, I stop. Even if it isn't the correct type of fabric I'm looking for, I appreciate its beauty by spending a moment with it.

I make my way through every aisle. The fabric store is bustling with busy people seeking supplies for their latest projects, but I ignore the other shoppers and do not make eye contact. I dismiss the old inner voice telling me that not seeking out conversation or making small talk with strangers is rude. Instead, I remind myself that if I ignore the need to remain vigilant to my internal harmony, I am not being authentic. If I am not faithful to myself, how can I teach Ashlynn to be?

I want to remain committed to my purpose. I am creating peace for myself. Authenticity is my self-care. My introversion is simultaneously my safe space and my happy place, and my purpose at the fabric store is part of my remedy for crafting a happy life. I will no longer shame it away.

I'm now at the last three rows of furniture fabric. I want something that looks and feels royal—material with a French provincial vibe that imitates a long-ago moment in time that has withstood centuries.

I find it. The pattern draws me in and I step toward it, my heart thumping. Its visual presence brings me joy. I stroke the roll of fabric—wrapped layers deep around a wooden pole. I pull her from the wall and head to the cutting table. There's no reason to continue searching. I have fallen in love. This is the one that will replace the decayed burnt orange, the bleeding red velour, and the rose garden on the green.

"How many yards?" asks the woman at the cutting counter. She reaches toward the fabric I'm cradling in my arms. I pass it to her.

"Six, please."

"What are you making?" she asks.

I swallow then stutter, "Um, a, um, I'm covering a couch." A simplified answer.

"Oh, that's going to be beautiful."

I smile. *I know*, I say to myself. I turn my back to the woman and pretend I'm looking for something in the button aisle. The vision of the fabric remains clear in my mind. It's a warm kind of blue mixed with the perfect amount of green to create a shade so soft it caresses your eyes with ease. The color must have a beautiful name, like Ocean Mist, Sea Foam, or Summer at the Lake. This calm, serene blue is embossed with a repeating pattern that reminds me of flowers but isn't quite floral. It's magnificent. The pattern feels imperial, like those present in fabrics made for emperors, kings, and queens—a royal tapestry, exquisite and stately.

I return home and head to the basement with two hundred and fifty-six dollars' worth of fabric. I clear a space on the floor large enough for cutting yards at a time. I sweep the dirt and dust aside, scoop it up into a dustpan, and flick into the wood stove.

I unroll the fabric over the seat of the settee—enough to gain a rough measurement of the first cut. I fold it at the respective place and move the material to the floor. I take a deep breath and make the first cut. The fabric is thick but soft. My scissors are sharp; there are no tears or pulls as I cut.

———

My therapy sessions started going smoothly, like the sharp scissors cutting through this new fabric. Each visit became another step in my quest for answers, and my therapist provided me with the knowledge to label and identify the wrongs done to me throughout my life. I learned about the causes and effects of what had happened. And suddenly, I could understand why I was struggling, and—more importantly—what I had been doing to cover my pain. My therapist could see me, and she validated everything. It helped me release my tension. And with each visit, I stepped out of another loosened rubber band.

I began taking a prescription for anxiety. The first one I tried was Prozac. It increased my panic attacks, which I started having in bed when I was trying to sleep. It also made me so full of energy that I stayed at the gym for two to three hours at a time. It wasn't a good fit.

Next, my physician prescribed Zoloft. The lowest dose was all I needed. It was like a light switch of anxiety had been turned off. Finally, she encouraged me to commit to therapy and not to reschedule my appointments if I began to dread them. She was right. I began to dislike bringing up the source of my pain. But I continued for five years, going once a week.

———

I plug in the air compressor and attach my pneumatic staple gun. The compressor hums as it builds with air pressure, readying itself for my project. I lay the cut piece of fabric over the foam of the new seat cushion. I eyeball the center, pull the fabric tight, and press the trigger on the staple gun. *Kapow.* Again and again.

The repetitive nature of stapling the fabric gives me comfort—comfort in the act of building something beautiful, like my own life. This artistic hobby of mine, along with writing, therapy, medication, and compassion, has saved my life.

I remember a time when I envied the people I watched in Portland's art district. From my perspective, they seemed happy because they were wise enough to know how to find happiness. Their relaxed, unaltered selves looked like the epitome of freedom. Hell, I don't know if that's how they felt. For all I know, they could have been covering their wounds, just like I was. But in their physical beings, I saw what I wanted. I saw something I didn't have. Many things I didn't have. Peace, happiness, safety, and love.

I have it now. It has taken fifty years of evolving for me to find myself.

My younger self's assumption of adulthood was that I would reach a higher level of happiness, having evolved past trivial hang-ups such as figuring out who I am, or trying to stay skinny, pretty, and confident. Oh, dear younger self, that was only the tip of the iceberg. I have finally figured out only a part of myself. I continue to attempt to stay skinny, and because my mother always said that pretty equals success, I shamefully do still care if I'm pretty.

The hum of the compressor restoring its air pressure reminds me that it's here for me, readying itself for the next staple. It is my steadfast and confident coworker.

I remind myself of my mother's words, "You're not confident."

I lived for years as a fake extrovert trying to prove her wrong. I was loud in my failed attempts to show her I was okay. I was rowdy, forceful, and desperate in my search for approval from anyone who would provide it.

I knew something wasn't right. I knew it felt off, but I had no idea why. As a teenager, I began observing other families—they ways they displayed love. Still, imperfect parents who disregarded what I looked like and welcomed me into their homes for days at a time gave me a new view of life, like my friends Pamela from Missouri and Kim from South Portland.

Life does not have to include self-loathing, addiction, blame, shame, poverty, and abusive behavior. I can embrace my truths, live my own life, and nurture my heart's desire for a happy home and a loving family.

I have only recently learned and accepted that I am an introvert. The career I have chosen is not one that nourishes my soul. I'm an office manager of an extensive dental practice, and I have an independent license for practicing dental hygiene.

I think of the famous saying about that elusive perfect career, "If you love your job, it doesn't feel like work." My ideal career is writing or anything requiring me to withdraw from the world and create while I visit with myself, like refurbishing an old piece of furniture.

I pull at the fabric securing it in a perfect line across the front of the seat. *Kapow, kapow, kapow.* In this pressed seam and the firmly planted staples, I rehearse and deposit my fifty years of growth—mainly how I have learned to protect myself from anything that doesn't instill peace in my psyche. I have consciously held on to a few rubber bands.

"I hate boats," I announce to the staple gun in my hand, as if it's listening. "This rubber band will stay. And I will allow myself to remain uptight about them. If I don't want to go on a boat, I won't guilt myself into it; I won't call myself a wimp or insult my experiences by ignoring my gut." The staple gun pushes my thoughts into each staple.

"I will also hold on to the rubber band of being a worried mother. It's the only kind of mother I know how to be. It's how I love. I know I will continue to have random panic attacks caused by non-evidence-supported suspicions that something terrible is happening to Ashlynn. My husband will remind me that she is okay and that no news is always good news with her."

I wipe the sweat from my forehead with my forearm as I move to the back of the couch. I pull against the fabric, smoothing out all the lines. Once it's tight and straight, I bend to my knees and ready the gun. *Kapow*—again and again.

To the back of the couch, I say, "I will overspend on Ashlynn at Christmas and dote on her when she is home. I will choose to spoil her over numbing my pain with poor choices."

A staple misses the wood, "Oh, sorry," I say to the love seat. With needle-nose pliers, I pull the loose pin out of the fabric.

"Another thing," I continue, "I have first-hand experience of what happens to a child when a parent chooses their vices, no matter how unhealthy, over the simple institution of parenting. The child will never fully recover. My struggles with low self-acceptance is a life sentence."

The staple gun pulls at the air built up in the compressor and accepts my declarations as fact, embedding them in the bond between fabric and wood. To undo any one of the thousands of staples would require a firm, twisting pull.

"I'm on my own clock, you know," I say. The couch has become a silent listener. The staple gun is my furious friend, willing to stab at anything I command.

"My clock, and my inevitable death someday, is not and will not be the same as my mother's. If there were a timekeeper for my life that marked decades and years instead of hours and minutes, mine would be ringing the praises of its fifty o'clock. The hour hand is replaced with a year hand and points at a mere five-oh, while the second hand—ticking along almost imperceptibly—measures months instead of minutes. There appears to be so much time left, but I am no fool." The compressor hums in agreement.

"I've often said that at age fifty, I'd be halfway to the end of my life. How is it that I believe I will live until I'm one hundred years old? It panics me to think any other way. After all, if I die at the same age my mother did, I would have been halfway through life at twenty-eight. And as of today, I'd only have seven years left. Or perhaps I'll die at the same age that my maternal grandmother passed–sixty-two. I would have been halfway there at thirty-one. My paternal grandmother was only forty, I think. Dying so young is absolutely unacceptable, horrible, and terrifying.

"Their spent their lives succumbing to abuse, jealousy, rage, cigarettes, and alcohol—basically a passive form of suicide."

I stand up to stretch my back. The staple gun remains on the floor. The house is quiet, and I am alone. I inhale and smile. I won't interfere with quiet moments like this by playing music or the television. Those are distractions from me connecting with myself. I will play music when I'm cooking, or when the family is around, or in the car. But that is it.

I return my eyes to the lovely couch. I take a deep breath and say, "This obsession with only being halfway there is part of my well-honed survivalist mindset. If I'm only halfway there, the mistakes, the lessons, the oh-shit moments are easier to shoulder. The trauma of my childhood will all have been for a better life later. Right? I will live the second half well-versed in who I am, and I will have learned what I require to be happy and prosperous. Right?

"Then why am I so worried? Yes, this worry came from the women before me who lived such short lives riddled with addiction, men who treated them horribly, and utter dissatisfaction with themselves. It also could be that my observations of human nature have opened my eyes to the masses of people who grossly misinterpret themselves as knowing better for everyone. Our brutally tunneled vision of self and minimal awareness of our impact on each other and our world horrifies me and nullifies my hope for a better second half."

I bend to the gun and move us to the right side of the couch. I pull at the fabric and begin following the next straight line. I tug at the material and secure it in place. *Kapow.*

"The greed for power and money, the devastation of our world, and the lack of safety living in it scare the hell out of me. And yet, like my child self, I must go on in the face of that paralyzing fear. It's a real-life nightmare.

"Checkmark survival skillset for fear of humanity—rationalize that the bad behavior of all of us is because we are still evolving. Slowly."

Kapow.

Chapter Seventeen

The Last Tack

As I continue talking out loud to my mother's love seat, I realize I'm verbalizing my thoughts and feelings to reinforce, to myself, where I am now and what I believe.

"Except for the people that love me, no one really cares how much I or anyone else struggles. Thank God for that, because I don't want to talk about it. And why should they care? They have their own families to worry about. I wish they would mind their own business and not even try. All of this pointless small talk somehow makes people feel better. I hate it. It's as irritating as styrofoam rubbing against styrofoam to me." I raise my eyebrows and shiver at the imagined sound. *Kapow*

"We are all struggling in our own individual ways. Others won't see my struggle because they haven't convinced themselves that everything will all be okay in their own lives. The act of outwardly projecting blame and a continued expression of detesting differing mindsets and lifestyles that don't align with our own is a fundamental hurdle that some human brains have not yet overcome because they haven't healed enough to move past those issues. I must continue to heal my hate and force my brain to fire different thoughts across synapses that have not only the ability but the desire to travel along new neural pathways, avoiding anguish and venom."

Pathways to love instead of hate, judgment, or intolerance.

"I fancy myself a cycle-breaker," I say to the inches of air between my face and the couch. I'm now on my knees, with sweat dripping down my neck as I pull at the fabric on the left arm of the sofa.

"I have also realized that my brain expects conflict. It was the primary state of my childhood home and my entire adult life until I met Billy. Hate and anger are what I exude when one of my needs is left unmet. If I feel fear, I become angry. If I feel jealousy, I hate. When I'm hungry, I'm mad. All of my anxieties exhibit themselves as anger and hate.

"Hell, if I'm not breaking cycles, then I'm still infected. If I'm still infected, that means I'm infectious. And that would be the worst thing I could be as a parent.

"If I can heal, anyone can. If I can find happiness, anyone can. If I can create a life exactly how I want it, anyone can."

I finish the left arm and move to the right. I fiddle with the fabric, trying to fit it even though I cut it too small. Pulling with all of my strength, "I can make it fit.". *Kapow.*

"As a child, Alcoholics Anonymous and Al-Anon meetings were necessary for my father's continued sobriety. I attended many meetings with him and my mother. I never spoke, but I listened. I learned about the trauma of other families. I was young enough that I felt like every story I heard became my own. And each wound felt real and significant to my life and safety. I could not understand how these people could allow a power other than their own to rule their lives.

"How could alcohol be so alluring? I didn't understand. As a kid, I wondered if I would find that one thing, like alcohol, that my life would revolve around. The answer is yes. Yes, I did—it was stress. But not anymore. Today, I'm happy to say that the one thing that rules my life is love.

"As a teenager, I developed a new survivalist skillset, so that when someone told me I couldn't do something, I made sure to prove them wrong. I played defense. Like on the field hockey team. The offense was meant for people who were good enough to score. They didn't need to defend themselves. They were good enough for God and good enough to be put on the front line where success was already in their hands." The staple gun produces another *kapow*, embedding my newfound strength into the straight line of the right arm.

"Now, I play offense in my life. I am the one on the front line trying to score. The trophy is happiness. I will forever defend my fears, but I won't allow them to hold me back from playing offense again.

"I have granted myself permission to grieve what I lost and to rest when my mind needs rest. If the pity-pot—a term I learned from my father's AA meetings—is where I need to be, then that's where I go. But I don't stay forever," I declare.

The pity-pot is a metaphysical place where a person sits and dwells in toxicity instead of purging it. Some people sit on the pity-pot their entire lives. Some take a short break from their otherwise optimistic outlook to hone in on, dissect, and remind themselves how much life sucks. A quick visit to the pity-pot can be helpful, like listening to sad songs after a breakup. It allows you to feel the shit. Embrace the shit and own it. Then, hopefully, you woman up and move on.

I continue to press the trigger, forcing staple after staple into the seams of the couch. I have a sense that I have healed something for my mother by finishing this. I imagine her huffing, "Finally." I look upon this imperfect piece of history with love and adoration. "How can I do the same for myself?"

I struggle daily with self-acceptance.

"I don't have a clue how to love my body, my hair, or my skin. How am I supposed to embrace fifty years old with a positive outlook? The delusions of my mentally ill mother still replay in my mind. She told me that youth is beautiful. And if you are gorgeous, everyone will love you. She said I could use beauty to get whatever I wanted in life. None of these are true. So what is true?

"I'm not young anymore. So must I be ugly and unlovable? The wrinkles, the sagging skin, the pigment from too much sun exposure, and my light green eyes that can barely tolerate any brightness. All figments of age and loss of youth and beauty."

As I move along the bottom edge of the back of the couch, I continue this conversation with myself and ask, "Who the hell is the genius who started that toxic self-hating cycle? Who told my mother this?" I ask, then I answer, "We cannot blame the media alone. Was it the twisted minds of lustful men and the weak minds of women who allowed it?

A superficial power trip for both? Was this the scope of their self-worth and search for truth and love?

"Well, I know my grandfather had a lot to do with it. That fucker commented on all the women in my family's bodies. He was insulting, mostly. Where the hell did he obtain that right?"

I laugh at myself and pat the dust from my knees.

"From here on out," I announce to the couch, the basement, the pneumatic staple gun, and myself, "I must remain intolerant to the stench and the trap of the emotional manure around me. It's thick with insults, oppression, and corruption. It will torment me into doubting myself and my worth. I must resist its blatant attack, no matter how quiet and sneaky. I will ward off the verbal bullets that attempt to embed self-hatred into my mind. Sometimes it's my own damn voice, sometimes a coworker, stranger, or family member. It may sound like words of concern or intelligence, but I must beware: their sole purpose is to pedestalize themselves while knocking me down to a place they're comfortable with.

"Like when Ashlynn was graduating from high school, I kept her plans to myself. I have built a very tall wall to protect my personal life. I never share. And yet so many people ignore that boundary and ask me personal questions. Like, 'What are Ashlynn's college plans?'

"Why? Why do they need to know? And every single person who wouldn't let up until I told them about her modeling plans would say, 'Well, she better have a backup plan.'

"That's like saying you're going to fail, so don't go toward that goal without planning on failure. I should have told these boundary crossers to get their pessimistic energy away from me." I pause to punch in a staple for emphasis—*Kapow*. "Who the hell are you to tell me or my brilliant daughter how to maneuver through life? Or warn us that we should plan on failure?

"Silencing my voice is sometimes necessary to shield myself from its brutality, alleviating its muddied shit. Yet, there are times when my voice is imperative to free me from its power, delivering me to my own. Knowing the difference is the challenge. Not blowing up at people is also a challenge."

I've spent hours on this project now, and I am feeling very accomplished and tired. The act of tightly securing each new piece of fabric gives me peace. The orderliness and precision in the steps ironed out many uneven moments in my mind.

"Alas, I am fifty years old, and yet I still dream about the most frightening and painful moments of my youth. One of the many recurrent nightmares I have is of driving a speeding car backward with my eyes closed and no brakes. I told my mother about this dream in my thirties, and she said that it had happened when I was a baby. She lost her breaks when she was backing up and ran into the side of a house.

"I dream of a home, the feeling of home, and the object of home. The house in this recurrent dream is one I have only seen in my dreams, and the feeling I have is one I am finally beginning to achieve in real life now.

"My favorite place to be in the world is home. I can travel within my home state without fear. But put me on a plane and I erupt in a feverish panic, terrified that I will die on this trip. Of course, I keep this swarm of anxiety inside because I know it's unlikely and Ashlynn and Billy love to travel. So I do it for them.

"When Ashlynn was a baby, my mother couldn't understand how I could stay home every night. On a weekly basis, she'd say, 'You need to get out of the house and do something fun.' I wondered if she was right. I worried that something was wrong with me because I didn't want to. Now I would have responded, 'No. No, I don't. To me, staying home with my baby is fun.'

"Another dream I have that began after Ashlynn was born is of being lost and unable to find her, or her needing me but unable to find me. And yet another is of my mother laughing at me.

"In real life, I struggle with the reality of these recurring manifestations of my sleeping mind. They hover alongside the difficulty I have with accepting my beauty and intelligence as enough. I over plan every moment of my life, and I am always afraid of being hungry. Maybe I have to accept all of these things—they're a part of me. This is me.

"Will I ever learn that love is beauty? Will I ever understand that love is where I will find happiness? Love for myself, first and foremost, then I can love others with my true authentic self." I stand up. I've had a lightbulb moment. "If I'm openly honest about myself with myself, then I can love authentically. Isn't that what I want?"

I put my right hand over my heart. The staple gun dangles

in my left. I look to the ceiling and, as if saying the Pledge of Allegiance, I make a promise to myself.

"I commit my next fifty years to serving love. Not only the hard work of improving my relationship with my husband every day and maintaining the purest form of love that I know for my wonderful child, but also loving me. I must accept my body, hair, and skin. I must choose a career that I love. Loving my home and spending as much time here as possible is easy. Loving my life and allowing others to love theirs is only fitting. I promise to limit my self-judgment to bettering my existence. I promise to press my awkward, insecure self to woman up and persevere.

"Love is beauty.

"I vow to embrace my world and who I have become. Ensuring I live past fifty-seven will also require a continued mindful approach to my physical and mental health. These are the kinds of beautiful things I want my daughter to see and emulate.

"I will break the cycle of shit with love.

"Hate is ugly."

I walk to stand opposite the couch. I stretch my chest toward the ceiling and take a deep breath. I inspect the sofa from afar and feel pride in my work. It's not perfect. I made mistakes here and there. I still find it beautiful.

"My life is not perfect. I am not perfect. But I am embracing the imperfections and finally living my life in an ideal way. I have worked hard for this. Since therapy, I have allowed myself to love and trust my husband. My daughter is thriving, and she comes to me when she's struggling. I continue to grow and learn about myself while I attempt to embrace every part—the good and the bad. It's a fight I am now ready to face every day.

"I remain dissatisfied with many aspects of my physical form. I dislike showing signs of age and will always remember my mother's words, 'Youth is beauty.'

"I pack food and water with me wherever I go, regardless of how short the time away from home is. I've decided that I worry about being hungry because of the scarcity of food in my youth, along with the decades of restrictions I placed on myself. Now that I am a well-fed adult, I worry about it. Go figure. I worry about Ashlynn being hungry too. And I accept this about myself.

"I worry about most things. I am fearful before something happens and after. I plan what I'll do and say so many times, rehearsing it over and over in my head, but when it comes time to act, I mess it up, and things never goes as planned.

"I find comfort in the routine of even the simplest of life's moments, like breakfast. I will eat the same thing for breakfast and my mid-morning snack for years on end. If I don't have these items in the house, I panic. 'What will I eat?'

"I provide myself with regular therapy by visiting antique shops, Goodwill, Salvation Army, and even yard sales. I adopt material objects into my home and family. I live my best life while I provide forever homes for artifacts given up from other people's lives.

"I seek refuge in renewing antique furniture, and I embrace the hope that the action of restoration provides."

I kneel beside the couch and focus on the final piece of loose fabric. I press my fingernails into the blue material and pull until it's tight. I have one staple left to sink. I wiggle the fabric into the perfect position, and I press the trigger of my air-powered staple gun. It misfires. No staple comes out. "Ha, of course," I say with a smile. My second attempt is a success. It's official—the antique love seat has new fabric. I run my palm over the seat cushion, appreciating the soft yet firm texture. I step back and look at her. She is beautiful.

I need to finalize the project with a finished edge treatment. I've chosen a combination of cording and head-to-head nails. The cording is a piece of rope that I will cover and sew with the same material.

I visit my mother's sewing machine, which I inherited after her death. I wrap four yards of braided cord with four yards of a one-inch-wide piece of the blue-and-gold fabric, and then I sew it together.

Since receiving this sewing machine, I have spent many hours with it. Mostly sewing ribbon and elastic on Ashlynn's pointe shoes. Her teenage dance career was life-changing for both of us. She learned the art of ballet by spending hours, days, weeks, and years perfecting her craft. Watching her dance was like witnessing a piece of artwork perform. She reached the elite level of ballet that only a tiny fraction of people do.

Every time I sit at this sewing machine, I have the same memory from my youth: the day my mother sewed through her finger. She made a lot of our clothes. We were poor. I remember the piercing sound of her screaming, "Tarzan, Tarzan, Tarzan," mixed with her hysterical screeching. The needle of the sewing machine went entirely through her fingernail and finger. Her finger was trapped, but her body jumped to standing, and she danced in pain until my father rotated the needle out of her teenage finger.

My heart races. I take a deep breath and begin sewing. I watch my fingers and jump every time the needle's cage hits one.

I spend two hours sewing the cording before I return to the basement. The love seat waits. I hot-glue the corded trim around the cut fabric edges—this is just one way of doing it. Some people sew the cord into the fabric before they cover the furniture. This finishing touch will cover the rough edges of the cloth, and the staples used to attach it.

Adjacent to the shining ebony-stained wood, I use tacks with a head-to-head nail technique. I hold each pointed tack with a pair of needle-nose pliers. I use the narrow head of my upholstering hammer to sink the point connected to a flat round head. Another repetitive task, yet somewhat less satisfying due to constantly hitting my fingertips with the hammer and the inevitable two out of four bent tacks.

Regardless, I persist through the difficulty of it. A lesson learned from my youth.

I would not trade the stories from my past for someone else's truths. They are mine. They belong to me, and they include the people that I love. My memories are mine and, of course, may not replicate someone else's who was present. Those are their memories.

"This story is mine."

After three hours of placing tacks into my newest family heirloom, I sink the last one. I raise my chest with a deep breath, and I smile. "Mom, your couch is done," I say.

I welcome all of what this couch means to me into my home—renewal. She is an armored safe holding my valuable possessions—memories, lessons learned, hope, and forgiveness.

Acknowledgments

This entire story acknowledges a broken family where each person lacks in the receipt and the offering of healthy love.

About the Author

Author, Tina L. Hendricks, was born in Bar Harbor, Maine. The Acadia National Park and Mount Desert Island were her playgrounds and safety nets from a violent home. She graduated cum laude with an Associate Degree in Science from the University of New England. Tina's love for storytelling began with her mother's vivid and youthful imagination who's power of make-believe in the midst of a brutal reality was a uniquely honed survival skill set that Tina adopted. Tina focused on her storytelling voice in high school with poetry.

Made in the USA
Middletown, DE
24 March 2022

63097713R00139